Manual For
Spiritual Maturity

bj King

1st WORLD
PUBLISHING

Manual for Spiritual Maturity

bj King

Copyright © 2025 by bj King

Published by 1st World Publishing
P.O. Box 2211, Fairfield, Iowa 52556
tel: 641-209-5000 • fax: 866-440-5234
web: www.1stworldpublishing.com

First Edition

ISBN Softcover: 978-1-4218-3585-3

LCCN: Library of Congress Cataloging-in-Publication Data

This material has been written and published for educational purposes to enhance one's well-being. In regard to health issues, the information is not intended as a substitute for appropriate care and advice from health professionals, nor does it equate to the assumption of medical or any other form of liability on the part of the publisher or author. The publisher and author shall have neither liability nor responsibility to any person or entity with respect to loss, damages, or injury claimed to be caused directly or indirectly by any information in this book.

What I offer to you in this book are my own opinions and beliefs based on direct experiences with Spirit over the past 40 years and information I've consolidated from reading Ancient Wisdom teachings. <u>These statements are not presented as THE TRUTH</u>. Do not accept what I have written as truth only as one person's opinion. <u>Accept only what resonates with your own discernment, your own truth</u>. Discernment is one of the spiritual gifts promised to us all. If you do not feel you have it, pray for it. All spiritual gifts are given to us as a result of our asking for them. <u>How you utilize the information in this book you do at your own risk. I accept no responsibility</u>.

Dedicated to

My Soul

Spiritual Hierarchy

Intergalactic Federation

All the people who have taken my classes

My Family

Table of Contents

1.

Meditation

Meditation and the gift of discernment are the two greatest gifts I've ever given myself and they both cost me nothing other than the willingness and the bravery to agree to know the purpose of my life. I consider direct soul communication to be the most valuable tool we can attain to live a sane, happy and spiritually directed life.

In 1978, I was living in Lubbock, Texas, married, Episcopalian Christian, mother and dedicated daughter. I took four Valium a day to maintain the level of commitments I had created for my life and the façade of perfection. I had constant headaches. I went to a dentist to be checked for TMJ to see if clenching my teeth was causing the headaches. The dentist made a retainer that kept my teeth from touching; I was to wear it while I was sleeping. On the third day of wearing it, I awoke to it being broken down the middle. I took it back to the doctor and asked him to glue it back together. He said he thought that wouldn't help; I was going to have to learn to relax. I had no idea how that was possible in my then lifestyle. He suggested I try biofeedback. I'd never heard of it. I asked who to go to and how much it would cost. He suggested it was usually administered by psychologists and most charged $75.00 an hour. Since my insurance would not pay for it, I left his office feeling hopeless.

When I arrived home my phone was ringing. The dentist explained that after I left he went into his office and there found a letter from a psychologist who had just moved to Lubbock from California and was looking to find ten TMJ sufferers for a trial study to see if she could help relieve the symptoms with biofeedback. The ten sessions would be free to the ten participants. I agreed to try it. He called and put my name on her list and made my first appointment. The first time I went, I was curious, but also doubtful, that this would help. The therapist asked me to sit in a recliner and hooked electrodes to the outside of my jaws. She dimmed the lights and sat beside me in another chair. She asked me to close my eyes and take a few deep breaths which I did, feeling increasingly more nervous. She then asked me to visualize and repeat to myself the number three, three times. My eyes instantly flew open and I demanded to know if the number was a Roman numeral or a regular number and what size and color it was to be. She laughed gently and said, "Make it up; it can be anyway you want it to be."

I was so insecure I needed her to tell me what to attempt to see, but she kept saying it didn't matter; I could use any visual that worked for me. I eventually settled on a regular number about four inches high and saw it as red and began to attempt to relax and breathe deeply. The machine I was attached to kept buzzing with an annoying high pitched sound. She then asked me to visualize and repeat to myself the number two, three times. I tried to follow what she wanted me to do, but the machine noise was distracting. She then asked me to visualize and repeat to myself the number two, three times. Next she asked me to visualize and repeat the number one three times, I followed her instructions to the best of my ability all the while being concerned I was doing it wrong because the machine would not shut up.

"Now, begin to count backward slowly from ten to one without visualizing anything. Just mentally count down," she suggested.

Down where I wondered? Where was I supposed to be going?

I never made the machine change sounds during the first session. I had no idea that what I was doing or trying to do was meditation. The second week the sound occasionally fluctuated and I felt it to be even more annoying and distracting than the constant buzzing. By the third week I was beginning to get the hang of it and felt more secure in my visualizing and counting. By the fourth week I would occasionally feel myself drift off almost falling asleep. I still never realized what I was doing was meditation. By the end of the tenth week my headaches were better and when I woke up with one I took time to go through the ritual of breathing and counting.

Years later, I quit taking the Valium and went through several experiences of the death of my Mom, my father moving another woman into my Mom's house eight weeks after her death, divorcing my husband and taking my children to Oklahoma where I intended to marry an Episcopal priest I had fallen in love with. He died of a heart attack four days after the move and my ex-husband came and took the children back to Texas to live with him. I was excommunicated from the Episcopal Church by the Bishop of Texas and the Bishop of Oklahoma. My friends turned against me because I had not lived up to their expectations. My reality crashed. I was left without an identity or roles to play for anyone. I went back into banking which was the only career I knew. In 1982, another series of events, including becoming unemployed, caused me to finally give in and completely turn my life over to God, agreeing that I would go anywhere, do anything and say anything God wanted if God would only talk to me. After this declaration I expected a big Charlton Hesston kind of voice to begin to speak to me, but there was nothing but silence. Disappointed, I went to a bookstore looking for a book on how to find one's life purpose. Being a good Christian I knew normally to avoid the occult sections of the bookstore, but that day I was so depressed that I walked right past it. A book flew off the shelf and landed on the floor right in front of me. I picked the book up and examined it. The cover was not attractive and the paper was newsprint quality. The name of the book was *Psychic Energy* and the author was Joseph Weed. I determined the book to be ugly, and ugly anything doesn't appeal to me, so I put it back on the shelf and went on to the self-help and religion section where I still felt my help should come from.

I found no book on how to find my life's purpose so I started back out of the bookstore and when I once again passed the occult section, the book that had previously fallen off the shelf was now lit up with a glowing light moving around it. I was amazed, frighten and dumbfounded. What could this mean? How could it have anything to do with me? I'm a very practical person and things did not light up in my reality at that time. I decided to take a chance and bought the book. On the way home I made a bargain with God that I would say a prayer, ask a question, close my eyes and open the book to one page the way we had been taught in the Church to seek divine guidance with the *Bible*. If the page I opened to made sense I would read only that one page; I did not want to subject myself to what the rest of the book might say. If the answer was not obvious and on that one page, I would throw the book in the dumpster.

I said the Lord's Prayer, closed my eyes and asked God to speak to me through this book. The page I opened to was a meditation to receive inspired writing from God, one's soul or higher self. I determined that this must be the guidance I needed and with much trepidation I decided to try it mainly because the meditation was almost identical to the breathing and counting that the psychologist had led me through during the biofeedback sessions. The visualizing and counting was the same 3,3,3,then 2,2,2, then 1,1,1 and counting down from ten to one. I took a shower to symbolically clear my aura even though I didn't really know what an aura was. I took the phone off the hook, sat on the couch in a loose fitting robe with my bare feet on the floor and paper and pencil on my lap.

My left brain just went crazy, "This is the dumbest thing you've ever done. This is not going to work. For God's sake put the phone on the hook and go get a job." I refused the suggestion, explaining to my brain that I had tried all that and it had not worked to make me happy or to satisfy me and that I wanted to know why I'm here or I wanted to leave.

After counting down and breathing, eventually there were words impressed on the right side of my brain, "Through this pen will come the words you need..." This phrase was repeated several times. I thought from the way the book described the meditation my hand would write by itself like automatic writing. After several repetitions of the same message I said aloud, "What?" The next set of five words was downloaded into my mind. I continued to write the words that came into my mind until I had filled seven legal size pages of writing.

The message asked me, now that I had turned my will over to God, to write out what I really wanted to do and where I really wanted to be. It also asked me to continue to meditate every day for thirty days before giving up. I was amazed by the information and wondered if I had made up the whole thing, but knew I would not set myself up to do anything for thirty days. I was later asked by my soul to take a course called *The Silva Method* by José Silva and found the same meditation used in that method. With *The Silva Method*, the instructor suggests we mentally create a laboratory and invite two spirit guides to join us there. The day I created my laboratory I invited two spirits I admired, Saint Francis of Assisi and Joan of Arc. They were useless to me as they had never met and spent my meditation time in the corner of the laboratory talking with each other. I later learned a better plan is to contact the highest level of your own Oversoul, during meditation through the Cosmic Christ Consciousness vibration that your body can tolerate and to invite and assign that level of yourself to be your gatekeeper or receptionist. Then if anyone else in the spirit world needs to communicate with you they first approach your gatekeeper who keeps away from you wayward spirits or spirits impersonating masters or higher level spiritual teachers. I've done the meditation daily for years and became very well acquainted with my soul and my mission using this meditation. I've been meditating for 40 years now and live in constant contact with my soul through deliberate soul infusion and even without going into mediation receive what it is I need to know.

I highly recommend if you choose to sit for meditation with this method or any other, you deliberately seal the room in which you are meditating on the North, South, East and West, the ceiling and the floor from any negative energies or entities because there are many lost souls wanting to attach to people who are still alive.

There are many forms of meditation; some take a person to the Alpha level of brain wave frequency, which is where this meditation takes you. Alpha is the most possible level to communicate with one's soul. Other forms of meditation take a person to Theta brain wave frequency, which is good for resting and rejuvenation, but is too deep for communication and makes it too easy to slip into Delta and to fall asleep, unless that is your intention.

It is not necessary to have a mantra or to sit in the uncomfortable lotus position to meditate. Actually any repetitive activity can be a meditation; walking, running, swimming, gardening, painting, sculpting, folding clothes, ironing, putting on makeup, shaving, doing dishes, sewing, knitting, crocheting, any form of creativity or driving.

Meditation is a gift we can give our body and our minds. It is the easiest way to release stress and to feel peaceful. When I go into mediation deliberately I always ask only one question, "What is the next single thing for me to do or know for me to be in a state of divine grace?" This question notifies our souls we are willing to have the next suggestion, the next assignment. Living in a state of receptivity, to the suggestions of my soul, causes me to have a peace I've never experienced in any other way. I always know where to be, when to get there and what to take with me. I'm willing to allow the soul to speak though me whatever the occasion calls for. Living this way makes me feel confident, peaceful and has relieved a great deal of the stress from my life.

THE SCIENCE OF MEDITATION

Torkom H. Saraydarian in his books *The Science of Becoming Oneself* and *The Science of Meditation* has much to recommend about meditation in scientific terms.

"Meditation is one of the greatest sciences that may save our planet from total destruction and make it a station of beauty though which Humans may contact the beauty of the Cosmos. It is the science of manipulation of energy, in accordance with the Will of the Cosmic Life." He also says, "Only through the right use, of the potent energies of the mind, will we be able to prevent total destruction and enter into the gate of the New Age."

His language is a bit different than mine, but the experience is about the same. Through meditating and contacting my soul, I've met members of my Oversoul, members of the Spiritual Hierarchy, Angels, and members of the Intergalactic Federation. I've gained memory of my life before I came into this life and found that my purpose is to serve as a liaison between these groups and Humans. I've taught anyone who has the will and tenacity to meditate they can learn their purpose for this life and where they were before coming into this incarnation.

Torkom also says: "Meditation in the New Age is creative thinking through the light of intuition and in conformity with the Divine Plan. In the New Age, meditation will involve not only the mystical efforts of Humanity, but it will involve, as well, the political, education, philosophic, artistic, scientific, religious and economic fields; it will create harmony within and between all these fields under the rhythm of the Divine Plan, of the Divine Will. Thus, meditation will be not only to gain insight, to contact great powers, to have inspiration and joy, but also to bring them down to practical life, to transform our life on all levels, healing the wounds of Humanity, building bridges and revealing the unity, the synthesis behind all creation."

I agree with him, meditation is the most practical way of bringing spiritual insights into our everyday life and as a means of finding solutions to our everyday challenges. Meditation does not just serve us spiritually; it is the most practical thing we can do for ourselves.

He also offers: "The purpose of meditation is to annihilate hindrances on the path of this expansion and to make you more aware of your cosmic relationships and of your cosmic destiny. Meditation leads you into freedom, and instead of being the slave of your egocentric viewpoints and cravings, you become a part of, one with, the cosmic viewpoint. Thus you help end the misery of all former civilizations: civilizations which grew out of Human tears, suffering, pain and blood."

"Meditation is a process of harmonization and attunement with the purpose of incoming energies from the higher realms and from outer space. Our civilization and culture is the result of our responses and reactions to the incoming energies. These energies may hinder our progress toward liberation if we are not ready to assimilate and translate them through our life and consciousness, or they may stimulate and release our inner glory if we are able to respond to these energies in pure compassion and in active service for our fellow Humans." It is important we understand our responsibilities, thoughts and actions affect the entire Universe.

"Meditation prepares us to become sensitive to these incoming energies. It enables us to be charged with them, and to translate them in the form of light, love and positive actions. This is how a New Age Human is born, a Human who is in tune with the purpose of the incoming energies and with the highest aspirations of Humanity.

"The soul is joy, and as we approach our Soul-consciousness we feel more joy, we radiate more joy. Those who do real meditation increase their joy, even if they live in the most trying of circumstances. And as they go deeper into their life of meditation, the losses and the gains of life do not affect them as severely, and their life as a whole seems to them as a play which they observe, in a detached way, knowing that nothing can harm them as far as they abide in the light of the Soul and radiate joy, peace and love.

"Meditation is a process of inner blooming, a process of charging your vehicles with spiritual energy. This energy regenerates your body, cleanses your emotional vehicle and purifies your mind, and as a result, your physical body looks younger and becomes energized, your heart enters into peace, and your mind gets sharper and more inclusive.

"It is a fact negative emotions wear out our body and worries, separative and selfish thinking cloud our minds. Meditation releases light upon those three levels and we start to regenerate our vehicles and radiate vitality, peace and serenity. Meditation makes you more able in your daily duties and works, because it increases your right judgment, sharpens your power of observation, increases your control over your body, quickens your actions and makes them more accurate.

"Meditation cleanses what you've stored in your subconscious gradually, to such a degree you are no longer the slave of your emotions and their effects. Because of this you do not leak energy, you waste no time, and you do your work better and in a shorter time.

"Meditation leads you to Soul-infusion. A Soul-infused personality is in tune completely, like a violin and violinist and the music. Then you have the stream of ecstasy radiating from the artist. Creativity is the result of such an attunement. No creativity is possible unless the Human is fused with the higher concepts, higher sources of beauty, and is able to bring these down to the physical brain, to their emotional world, and give birth to them as some kind of art.

"Meditation aligns and tunes up all vehicles and fuses them with the Inner Source of light, love and power. It causes one to have a living beauty, and to become a server of the Human race, an example of a path through which Humans may achieve.

"Meditation helps us to formulate our thoughts and to build a structure of our thought forms, with finer substance, in great harmony with the note of divine ideas, and to create a corresponding life of beauty."

Our goal in meditation may be to align our will with the will of our soul and our I AM Presence. By doing this, we create a bridge which serves as a communication line between the intuitional plane, the mental plane and our physical brain.

It is extremely important we become aware of our thoughts, feelings and emotions and to understand we have the power to control and change all of these. It is easier to do once we have the conscious assistance of our soul through soul communication. It is important to understand the information given to us by our souls is not an order, but merely a suggestion, and the soul, God, will never take away our free will even when we deliberately turn our will over to God.

Our goal needs to be to listen vertically before we act horizontally.

Thinking means to create, to be. That is why it is very important to know how to meditate, how to create pure and divine thought forms to increase vitality and health for onesself, Humanity and nature.

2.

Surrender Into Freedom

I personally have always disliked the words "surrender, discipline and frugal". I always thought of surrender as a weakness. Even though I was very involved in religion, I had never completely surrendered my will to God. I was afraid God would expect me to go to Africa to be a missionary. In 1982, when there had been so much loss in my life—my mother, my father, my children, my husband, my home, my job, my fiancé—I was willing to give up my life to death. When suicide didn't work, I agreed to surrender my life to God. I had never completely surrendered my life to God, even though I had pseudo surrendered by doing everything the Episcopal religion required of a surrendered person, short of becoming a missionary. The day I said to God, "I'll do anything you want; I'll go anywhere, do anything, say anything you want, if you will just talk to me." I, of course, was expecting a Charlton Hesston kind of voice to speak to me.

Because of the strange circumstances of the book, *Psychic Energy* being thrown off the shelf at me at the book store, when I meditated the information did not come as a voice, but rather as words placed into my mind on the right side of my brain. The information came five words at a time, giving me time to comfortably write them down. The criticizing thoughts on the other side of my brain did not stop, but said, "This is the dumbest thing you have ever done; for God's sake, put the phone on the hook and get a job."

Through the years I meditated and made an effort to follow the information I received in meditation. At first I thought the assignments were orders from God and I had to follow them to the best of my ability, regardless of the expense. It was years later, when I threatened to quit following the information and go back to being a banker, so I could at least receive a pay check, the writing explained the assignments were only suggestions coming from God through my soul and that I still had my Freewill and could say "no" or to write "conditions under which I could do this for you." At that time I had $26,000 in credit card debt at 21% interest. My soul convinced me I could become debt free if I wrote out my debt in detail and released it to the Universe to be settled through Divine right action. I didn't believe this was possible, but I did what was suggested and, within a few weeks, I was gifted with $1,000 in cash, along with a $25,000 CD left to me from a friend who died.

From that time on I learned to negotiate with my soul. I still follow the guidance to the best of my ability, but I've learned I am expected to write out my desires about my physical life and the soul and I, if I follow the suggestions, can co-create a life of joy, freedom and satisfaction. I no longer look at surrender the same way. I now know I AM surrendering to that which created the body and that part of who I AM knows what is best. There is a sense of freedom in this surrender because, if I follow, I have the peace that comes from always knowing I AM at the right place, at the right time, with all I need to bring with me and I AM willing to allow my soul to speak through me to say whatever the situation requires.

There are three levels of understanding that have a direct impact on our well-being in the Universe. The lowest level of understanding pertains to our immediate survival, with little perception or recognition of consequences. Living from survival consciousness may satisfy short-term necessity, but it can lead to bitter traps, confusion, anxiety, depression. The next level of understanding is that of cause and effect, which leads to decent, civilized behavior with significantly more command of life. If we stop at this level, however, life will be dominated by structure, linear logic, control and judgment. Life will be very limited. Fortunately, there is a Third and higher level.

SURRENDER TO WHOLENESS AND FREEDOM

Jesus says: *"The highest level of understanding involves surrendering to the power of wholeness which is all-inclusive. This final level of surrender requires a great leap of faith and consciousness, for it is truly where faith and consciousness rule. Both faith and consciousness are required in great measure, as well as love, acceptance and forgiveness.*

"All three levels of understanding are needful and valid. It may surprise you that some people need to be taught to survive, or helped in doing so.

Others need a refresher course in cause and effect. Nevertheless, everyone would be wiser to understand that infinite wholeness has the power to utterly command life, shatter it, or rebuild according to patterns of greater good. When one is attuned to that power through love and synchronicity, separation of God and Humans will cease, and life will be filled with greater blessings, broader understanding and conscious immortality."

My life and reality were shattered between 1979 and 1982. The conscious surrender to God and beginning to follow the soul's suggestions has rebuilt my life into patterns of greater good and peace. Leaving religion for spirituality has brought me peace and a sense of satisfaction with my life I never felt while I was involved with religion.

Spirituality is the music of the Universe, while religion is a dance we devise to limit infinity to structure. Surrender to unity, to Oneness.

As long as we see ourselves as separate from God, the Cosmos, other people, the Universe, other creatures, we will feel fear, insignificance and doubt. Once we **remember**, we are aspects of God and that we are a part of everything that exists, we will feel useful and begin to understand and remember why we are here at this time.

SURRENDER TO KNOWINGNESS

It is my experience when people first begin to wonder about spirituality, they read lots of books and listen to other people. Most of the books I exposed myself to suggested I should expect to see and hear spiritually as well as attempt to communicate with my "guides." So, of course, I tried that, even though I was already in communication with my soul. I later learned seeing spiritually is possible in the Third and Fourth dimensional energy. Spiritual hearing is possible in the Third, Fourth and Fifth dimensional energy. Most of us who are here now came from higher realms of energy to assist with what is going on during this stage of evolution of Earth, Humanity and all creatures on the Earth. We came from silence and knowingness. It is time for us to remember this and to ask our souls for knowingness. Many people hesitate to have complete knowingness because to know eliminates our right to excuses. Trust me; to know is worth giving up our excuses.

SURRENDER TO LOVE

God is Love. At our core we are made from Love. Humans more often think of love in romantic terms, with romantic fantasy. The type of Love that is the Love of God can be experienced in many forms: (from *The Book of Love* by Kathleen McGowan, author of the *Expected One*)

Agape – a love that is filled with the joy of each other and for the World, a purest form of spiritual expression; here is the sacred embrace that contains consciousness.

Philia – a love that is first a friendship and full of respect; the love of blood siblings and true companions; here is the sacred embrace that contains trust.

Charis – a love that is defined by grace, devotion, and praise for God's presence in the chambers; this is where the love of our mother and father is found, on Earth as in heaven.

Eunoia – a love that inspires deep compassion and a commitment to the service of the World and all God's people; this is where our love for charity and community lies.

Eros – a love that is a profound physical celebration to which the souls come together in the union of the bodies; this is the ultimate expression of beloveds, when it is experienced with spiritual intention. <u>It is important for us to designate a place for the orgasmic energy to go. If we do not mentally designate it to healing someone specific or to manifest an item we desire the expressed raw sexual energy adds to the possibility of rape or sexual abuse if it is just expressed into the ethers</u>. Sexual energy is a strong energy for creation. Used correctly it creates another Human.

The one great commandment that Jesus left us with is to love God above all else with all our heart and soul and to love our neighbors as ourselves.

SURRENDER TO KINDNESS

To be kind costs nothing. The choice to consciously choose kindness as a path will change your life. In every opportunity, when there is a possible choice to be kind, to be cruel, to be fearful, to be angry, to disagree, to avoid, to ignore, to be indifferent, remember to surrender to kindness.

SURRENDER TO COMPASSION, NOT EMPATHY

Compassion is different than empathy. When we are empathic we go to the level of the emotions of the other person. At that level we are not helpful to them, we are "in it" with them. If we feel compassion we are combining the level of our soul's passion with the level of their soul's passion and bringing them the energy of their own soul to lift them into clarity and peace.

SURRENDER TO WEALTH

To be poor, whether in spirit or financially, does not serve us, others or the Universe. We are called to be co-creators with God and the Universe. The way we are made in the image and likeness of God is that we are designed to be creators. To have wealth, energetically, physically and financially, and to use it spiritually, is our divine mission.

SURRENDER TO WISDOM

There is a difference between knowledge and wisdom. Knowledge can be gained from books and lectures, from education, but knowledge is useless until it is turned into wisdom through experience. To know a thing, but to have no experience of the thing, is not wisdom. Wisdom is only gained through experience. We cannot be spiritual through knowledge. We can only gain true spirituality through our own experience of God, the Universe and Oneness.

SURRENDER TO SERVICE

We are here to be the hands, feet, voice, and mind of God. Our bodies were created by our souls as vehicles through which our soul, through inspiration from God, can be of service to the planet and all its inhabitants. We are to be servants in service to the Divine Plan of the Creator of All Universes. You are allowed to choose the form your service will take. Each person has different gifts to offer. When we are using our gifts in service we have an opportunity to feel bliss, satisfaction and joy. We know we are serving our mission; we are being God in Human form.

SURRENDER TO RECEPTIVITY TO YOUR SOUL

Our ego wants to believe it is in charge. It wants us to feel fear of surrender to the soul, because it feels loss of control. It has a purpose and that is to warn us when we are considering doing something that will destroy the body. When we surrender to the soul, the personality and the ego begin to be adjusted by the soul to feel less fearful of losing control. The knee jerk reactions, the anger, fear, judgment and anxiety begin to be dissolved.

SURRENDER TO THE TRUE SELF YOU ARE

Our true Self is God incarnate in Human form. Once we begin to remember "I AM God operating through this personality for the benefit of Earth, all life on the Earth and beyond," we know our true selves. We know our mission; we know the next single thing to do or know. We know we are not our bodies. We know our bodies are the garments our soul wears in order to show up on Earth as a Human to do the will of God.

SURRENDER TO THE MYSTERY

At all times we can choose to surrender to our history and to live from the past and our false beliefs about who we are as a result of that history; or we can begin to remember the truth of who we are and live in the mystery of not having to know the future, but trusting because we are surrendered to God, our souls, the future will be what we think, believe and expect as co-creators with God and the Universe.

SURRENDER TO THE TRUTH

We are the children of God. We are loved beyond our ability to understand how much God cares for us as His own creations. We are born to be God in the disguise of a Human to bring the energy of the Cosmic Christ Consciousness to Earth for Humanity and the Earth, at this time, to aid in the evolution of Earth's and Humanity's mutation into the Fifth dimension. We are here to serve as conduits for this energy to bless the Earth and Humanity. We are here to enjoy the process. We are here to live in joy, love and beauty and to bring the Age of Enlightenment to Earth.

LOVE IS THE ULTIMATE POWER,
IT RESIDES IN SURRENDER TO GOD.

When you think about the word "surrender" and consider doing it, I think it is useful to remember that you are not surrendering something that was even originally yours. The soul created the body for its use. Our egos took on ownership. We were always eventually expected to remember that we are not our bodies, but we are part of the soul that created the body for its use.

Opening myself up to Divine guidance, allowing the Divine to express through me in my life...the concepts both frightened and thrilled me at the same time. For the first time I was open to the reality I was never in control to begin with.

Unexpected opportunities began appearing in my life. I said yes. Sometimes the opportunities were disguised as challenges. I said yes. Sometimes I went kicking and felt I was being dragged, but I said yes. I learned God has a greater plan for my life than I could ever have imagined.

I felt like I was going along pretty well and one day in meditation I was told "You must surrender more." Well, you talk about livid. I had given up my husband, my home, my profession, my parents, my friends, my fiancé, my children, and all my belongings except what would fit in the car. What else could God possibly be expecting me to give up? "Your fears, your doubts, your disbelief, your anxiety, your limitations, your resistance, your resentments, your expectations, your anger, your grief," was the response.

I think some of the most difficult things, for me to get used to when dealing with the soul, are I am a curious person, I have a "need to know" and I <u>really</u> like to feel in control. The soul is often cryptic in its messages, in my opinion, but I have learned to be belligerent and demanding and we have come to some agreements about my need to know. I have learned that not trying to be in control, but allowing the soul to point the best direction, works better than my wanting to figure everything out while trying to control people and outcomes. I'm not always allowed to know the future or to know why I need to show up in a certain place at a certain time, but so far I've been cared for, protected and supported.

I was once asked to go on a Mexican Caribbean cruise by myself with 2,500 other people who I did not know. I went and I learned one good phrase during the week. "It is what it is."

Eckhart Tolle says, "Surrender to what is. Say yes to life and see how life suddenly starts working for you rather than against you."

I have learned to surrender thinking my conscious intellect has all the answers and to instead understand consciousness conceives, governs and constructs the Universe. And the Universe is as infinite as the Mind of God.

There are many ways we use our minds throughout the day. One of the most common is what I call "automatic pilot." This occurs when we let habitual thinking run our day. What will I eat? What will I wear? Should I stop for gas? There is no original thinking at work when our mental habits drive us.

There are spiritual practices that can take us out of ordinary run-of-the-mill kind of thinking into deliberate uses of the mind for the purpose of being more open to Infinite Mind. According to metaphysical belief, there is only One Universal Mind, and everything and everyone that thinks uses this Mind. The ultimate desire is to be attuned to this Mind and able to access its wisdoms and healing powers for ourselves. Simple enough, but ordinary thinking does not usually get us very far. Spiritual practices do, and one of the best is the often misunderstood use of the concept of surrender.

Most things aren't under our control anyway. The flow of life brings change, whether we like it or not, so we can either fight what comes or work with it. This is where surrender can come in. We can choose to give over rather than to give up or fight what is happening. The practice of surrender can open the channel to our higher consciousness. Often, if we have a problem and let it go and ask for an answer to come while we are sleeping, or go do something that takes our mind off the problem, a solution will come.

Surrender can and is often a difficult practice to grasp because we feel like we are giving up something or we fear the unknown if we give up control. But actually surrender isn't about giving up' it is about becoming more. We are always more than any role or label we accept or play. We are the Divine Itself manifesting as the unique individualization that we are. Surrender, then, is not giving up or giving in. Rather, it is stepping aside and allowing the Divine so fully into our consciousness that our life is taken over by Its Presence.

Whatever we do not surrender eventually binds us. If we practice surrender of conditions as we know them on a regular basis, when changes come we will be able to release them without such a terrible wrench, but with a greater sense of understanding. Mental surrender does not have to be a gut-wrenching, last-ditch effort to free ourselves from some troubling concern. If we are wise, it will be one of our first moves so we can be available to the Infinite Mind right away. The sooner we use surrender as a personal choice, the sooner we are free to receive the response the Divine Mind always has for us.

Flow is a word I like to use. I like to imagine myself in a state of easy movement that carries me through my days in the best and most fruitful way. The only way I have learned to allow this to happen is to stay in the moment asking my soul only, "What is the next single thing for me to do or know for me to be in a state of Divine Grace?" And to follow the knowing that comes to me from my soul after the question.

We often hang on to the status quo until we are literally forced to surrender to something greater. We believe we can handle it. What we know is more attractive than what we do not yet know even if it is painful or unrewarding. Our egos want to exhaust our Human resources before we'll give it over to the Presence of God.

**THERE IS NO ACTUAL SEPARATION BETWEEN THE SACRED
AND THE SECULAR EXCEPT IN OUR OWN MINDS.
EVERYTHING IS SPIRITUAL.
GOD IS THE GIVER AND SUSTAINER OF ALL LIFE
AND EXPRESSION.
GOD IS ALL THERE IS. GOD IS SUBSTANCE AND SUPPLY.**

God does not take our free will. We must surrender before God can work in our lives. Surrendering doesn't mean giving up, it means, we can draw upon something more powerful than everything else we've been depending upon. We did not make our own being. All we can do is to accept, the being which we are, is some part of the Divine. Everyone surrenders sooner or later if you consider death as the ultimate surrender.

Say yes and allow God to express greatly in your life. Let go of how you think things should happen and allow God to be God.

3.

The God Within

Eastern spiritual systems have for millennia proclaimed Oneness, the unity of all things, rather than separation as Western science has presented truth until recently. Quantum physics has now demonstrated the unity of body and mind is actually the truth of our existence. Mind and body are one inseparable entity, together forming the whole of who we are. From the tiniest atomic particle to the largest planet, from the smallest cell to the most immense galaxies, everything exists together in an infinitely intricate web of interconnection. What affects one part affects all the rest, even though the majority of the changes are so minute that we cannot perceive them.

Earth and Humans are a part of a living system that embraces everything and we all participate in "a universe of consciousness." We generally assume that the solutions we are seeking come from outside ourselves, but it's important that we shift to an internal recognition that problems come from within ourselves, as do the solutions. In other words, it's all about consciousness. We typically think of consciousness as our thoughts or cognitive processes. But it's so much more—actually the Source of all that is.

Consciousness is not just about Humans. It's about the great unfolding of the nature of reality. It is a process by which we are able to have self-reflection, awareness, and are able to self-correct.

Consciousness exists on various levels. For instance, our bodies are conscious because they can self-correct without our being aware of it—they do so all the time by regulating our temperature, fighting off microbial invaders and so on. Yet, when we become aware and use intention we can direct consciousness through our mind-body for healing.

Whatever we mentally see and spiritually comprehend, we may objectively experience, for the God consciousness within us is not limited to any one experience. It is the Creator of all experience.

Nature is a conscious system. It, too, has many feedback loops that produce self-reflection, awareness and self-correction. We would do well to have reverence and awe for the innate intelligence in nature. A lot of what is problematic is about Human intervention.

Our Worldview is one aspect of consciousness, individual and social. It is the way we perceive the World around us and interpret what we experience. A Worldview consciousness combines beliefs, assumptions, attitudes, values and ideas to form a comprehensive model of reality. In our Worldviews, we construct complex conceptual frameworks to organize our beliefs about who we are and the World we live in.

Our awareness, of how much these influences rule us, is generally hidden from our conscious mind. This means we operate in default mode most of the time. Our neural pathways become entrenched, creating mostly unconscious habits that lead us to think and behave in the same way over time—not a good recipe for creating positive, sustainable change, whether we want to quit smoking or eliminate war.

How can we become aware and break free of this cultural hypnosis rather than just being victims? Rather than seeing nature as something we have a right to attempt to dominate we can move to an awareness of nature as consciousness and protect it and agree to work in harmony with it. We need to see ourselves and nature as a part of God in order to maintain a Worldview transformation. The answers lie in shifting our attention from external to internal forces. Positive transformation of our Worldview is the only thing that will save us and the planet.

There is a great difference in whether or not we believe God to be within us or outside us. For if God is outside us, how are we going to reach this God, who, not being some part of us, must be separated from us? How can we hope to unite things which are different from each other? The God who is already within us, being forever perfect and complete needs no reunion with anyone and we need no reunion with this God, because this God is in our every cell, every act, in every thought, in every movement, in our every plan, purpose, and performance. The God within us creates every circumstance and situation we have ever experienced. We have called these circumstances and situations things in themselves, but they never have been. They have always been the fruition of our thought, and our thought has always been dominated by our belief in God ever since we had self-conscious life. The experiences reflect if we believe and communicate with a God within us or a God on a cloud somewhere judging us.

The life within us is God; whatever is true of God is true of our lives, since our life and the life of God are not two, but One. The enlightened have ever proclaimed this unity of good, this Oneness of Humans with God. For this reason, many have spoken of this Life within us as both personal and impersonal. Impersonal from the stand point It is universal—personal from the standpoint this Universal Life Principle is personified in us.

This life within us, being God, did not begin and It cannot end, hence we are immortal and eternal; that is, we can never be less, but must forever be more of ourselves; as this Life within us unfolds through our experience, through our gathering of knowledge and our accumulating of wisdom. Evolution is the drawing out of the God-Principle already latent within us.

The God that is within us is truth, beauty, harmony and wholeness. Every apparent imperfection from which we suffer is a result of ignorance. Because ignorance of the Universal Law excuses no one from its effects, it follows that the very power which has bound us, rightly understood and properly used, will produce freedom.

The God within us is unity and not duality. The very fact this Unity is changeless, forever revealing Itself to each is why the God, who is already within is harmonious and perfect, has ever appeared as the God we believe in. We might say the God within, being infinite, appears to each one of us as the God who is believed in. And we worship the God whom we believe in, rather than the God who is. But there is nothing wrong about this, since the God which is believed in, is at all times, some part of the God who is. Therefore, whatever God you believe in, provided you believe this God is already in you, and must respond to you at the level of your belief. This is why it is done unto each one of us as we believe. The Principle is infallible; the practice is what we make it.

Ever since we have had self-conscious thought, we have by our use of the Law of Liberty, created bondage. Not that bondage really existed, but the possibility of using freedom in a limited way existed. We really never bound freedom; we merely used it in a restricted way. The restriction was not in the Principle, but in our use of it. There is a difference whether you believe in actual limitation, or merely in a restricted use of freedom. If limitation were a thing in itself, you could not change it, but since it is merely an outline of experience, why not use our imagination to enlarge change the experience? When we do this, we will find the Life Principle within us responds just as quickly to a broader outline. The old outline was imaginary only, never real. It was like the horizon where the Earth and sky appear to meet, but as we travel toward this apparent wall, we find it disappears.

Emerson said there is One Mind common to all individual Humans which, of course, means the Mind of all Humans is the One Mind which each uses; therefore, the Mind which you use is the Mind which I use. It is the Mind which everyone uses. It is the Mind of God and because the Mind of God is a complete unity, it is omnipresent. Therefore, the Mind which we use and which is our mind now is the God-Mind in us—this Mind is in all of us, and is the center of everything. This is why when we know the Truth at the center of our own being; we know it within the only Mind there is. The Mind that we possess at this moment is the Mind which Jesus used to demonstrate the Christ Principle and to accomplish miracles. He must have realized God is at the center of His being, and it is a realization of this Mind of God, at the center of our being, which gives power to our words.

Since the Mind within us is the Mind of God, and since the Mind of God has been in all Humans, then it follows that the intelligence within us understands what the great teachers of the past have talked about. We already have within us an understanding, comprehending mind. The Mind of God has no problems, no difficulties, and is never confused. Therefore, our real mind has no problems, knows no difficulties, and is never confused. It is our intellect which is confused. When we know that the Mind within us is God and cannot be confused, our intellect becomes clarified.

This Mind, which is God, permeates every atom of our being. It is the governing Principle in every organ of our bodies. It is the Principle of Perfection within us. The Principle is perfect, complete and limitless, but our thought circumscribes its action and causes the very Mind of Freedom to create conditions which you call bondage or problems. As we teach our intellect to believe in free circulation of Spirit through us, our thoughts become a law of elimination to congestion, it purifies stagnation. Our consciousness of the Divine Presence within us, like light, dissipates the darkness. This is our eternal and true self at the center of our being. It is the Mind of God manifesting Itself in us, as us. This "us" which It manifests is not separate from Itself, but is Itself. This Invisible Presence is the Cause of the Light shining through us.

We and our ego create our personality. It is useful to turn our personality back to God and to ask to become "soul-infused personalities" in order to make our bodies and mind more useful and our souls more useful to God.

The Divine and Infinite Mind, always desiring self-expression through us, is an insistent urge, compelling us to move forward. The Mind in us is also in all people. When we recognize other people, it is this Mind knowing itself in them. The Mind within us is timeless, yet It creates all periods of time. It is the intelligence behind of every action, whether we call such action good, bad or indifferent. It is always creating form, but it is never limited to any particular form. It is in our every act, but It is always more than any or all of our actions. Even though we appear to be bound, the Mind within us is perfectly free.

Our intellect in no way limits this Mind merely because it conceives of what we call a small form or a little space. It could just as easily conceive of what we call a large form or a bigger space. In other words, our intellect is doing the best it can with the Mind within us. It reflects this Mind, but not completely. We are this Mind in action and the enforcement of Its Law. This Law is the Law of our Divinity, and since we are an individual, we manifest this Law in a unique way. We project this Mind through experience in a personal manner, different from all others. This constitutes our true and immortal self.

Since the Mind within us is the Mind of God, and since the Mind of God not only created everything that has ever existed, and will create everything that is ever going to be, we already have within us the ability to project new ideas, new thoughts, new inventions. Therefore, whatever ideas we desire, when we pray—that is when we listen to this inner Mind— we can know that we are going to receive these ideas, for we are dealing with that Mind which is the Conceiver of all ideas. When we call upon this Mind for a solution to our problem, at once It knows the solution because there is no problem to It. In this way, the solution to every problem is in the Mind which we possess because we are the children of God.

4.

Trusting Your Immortal Soul

We are each indivisible, immortal souls and cells in the totality of the universal organism called God. Each soul is both a particle and partner of Spirit. We are particles of Universal Life Force. As such, we have a responsibility to add to the energy of God through our thoughts, actions and intentions. We are agents of divinity responsible for infusing divine energy into the physical realm. We are here for a purpose; to infuse love into everything we think, feel, sense and encounter and, thereby, transform and uplift the Earth and all life on the Earth. We are here to further develop and express our divine consciousness as we add to Spirit's continuous creativity.

In the past, before we recognized ourselves as aspects of God and immortal souls, most of us joined organizations that rendered us vulnerable to the needs and wishes of anyone willing to fill our desire for truth about God with their beliefs, preferences and perceptions.

It took many of us a long time to realize an infinitely Loving God is much too big, too inclusive by nature, too compassionate in practice, too multi-dimensional in reality, to ever be contained within the constructs of any one historical institution.

We are divine souls here on Earth, living the outline of a script and contract we composed and agreed to, with our Oversoul, before we assumed our current physical form and took up residence in the mind and body we chose for this lifetime's incarnation. We are each translating the outlines of our contract into a lifetime of specific choices. When we choose to incarnate, we also choose the outline, characteristics of our placement, parents, talents, dysfunctions, perspectives, body type, challenges and dominant issues and patterns of our life. Once incarnated, however, we make our specific choices within that outline of intentions, consciously and unconsciously choosing to support them, negate them or ignore them. We are responsible for creating our life progressively from outline to specific details. We will attract to us the people, circumstances and challenges we need to manifest our desires and intentions. We are free to fulfill, modify or negate what we chose earlier as our learning objectives because we always retain our Freewill. Each incarnation is designed to help the Soul develop its potential to become whole and indivisible, like God.

Choosing a life on Earth as a Human is considered one of the most difficult assignments a soul can choose because of the complications and complexities of Earth and Humanity. It is difficult to deal with the polarities of time and space, masculine and feminine, reason and emotion, spirit and matter, and life and death. Earth is cosmically considered a learning laboratory in which Humans are given the opportunity to infuse divine love into every image, interaction, intention, experience and situation. We have incarnated on Earth to have a material, Earthly and spiritual experience, simultaneously.

We all have egos. Until the ego has done its work by giving direction and energy to getting the incarnate established in the World as a distinct and stable or successful individual, it is unlikely to be willing to relinquish its leadership role and allow itself to respond to the promptings of the soul. Often, this does not happen until middle age or when the physical needs of the individual such as food, shelter, housing and income have been established. The ego believes its role is to keep us from harm. It also believes, if it relinquishes its hold on the mind of the body, that the being will destroy the body. It takes coaxing to get the ego to cooperate with the soul rather than to keep running the show.

We are an integral part of a spiritual collaboration that includes God, you, me, the Angelic Hierarchy, the Avatars, the Intergalactic Federation, the Spiritual Hierarchy of our Universe, Master Teachers, and every living consciousness and Soul entity that exists in our entire Omniverse (a collection of 12 Universes). We are co-creators with all these beings in the continual unfolding of the Omniverse. Our intentions and actions help to enhance the spiritual evolution of our planet and, in so doing, support the process of bringing more and more of heaven to Earth.

You are more than your body. Everything depends on how you define yourself. Your life is not really over when you surrender your body to physical death. Your immortal soul lives on. Your immortal soul willed and formed your current body and incarnation is available to guide it every minute of every day. Contacting our soul and asking for direction is the sa nest thing we can do. Our souls seek recognition. Without soul contact, we take a chance we may not fulfill our contracts, our missions.

Everyone you have and will ever meet is also an immortal soul. Souls all rotate onto Earth in order to complete missions related to the themes of love, enlightenment and to attain a fuller awakening to our spiritual nature.

The recognition of your spiritual identity as an immortal soul may have been stirring in you for years, but you may have denied it perhaps because of the fear of being thought audacious or presumptuous by embracing such an empowering enormity. Most of us suffer bouts of temporary amnesia during our stays on Earth. We forget who we really are and believe we are our bodies and minds.

It is important we move beyond believing we are just our bodies and remember we are aspects of God, operating through these personalities, and, as such, have a responsibility to the totality of Earth, the Universe, Humanity and God. We are to be conscious co-creators with God, with our souls.

Humans are divine souls having an Earthly experience
in order to deepen and expand our capacity to love.

We have all had, and will continue to have, multiple lives or incarnations to make our contributions and to have infinite opportunities to bring God's essence of love and compassion into material form. Having multiple incarnations to attain our goals and develop our spirituality is not an excuse to relax. We are to do the task in front of us; not to rush it, but to do it right. As an immortal soul, we provide a direct connection between the spiritual realm and our everyday material realities. Intention and action are what moves the World; it is what transforms an idea into a reality. This is also true of the intention to have soul communication. It is impossible not to have soul contact, for our bodies belong to our souls. It is possible to avoid soul communication, however. Receiving soul communication is a choice.

Our health, the incredible functioning of our brains, the continual pumping of our hearts, the continual rebuilding of our cells, the presence of our families, our jobs and careers, and our capacity to delight in our favorite foods, all exist, all function, all are possible because of the presence, significance and love of our souls.

At the time of the death of our physical bodies, we surrender our bodies and move back into the realm of Spirit. We review and evaluate our progress, after which we resume our studies and prepare to choose, when the time is right, one more incarnation; one that serves both the needs of our individual soul as well as the loving intent and creative preference of the entire Oversoul. We exist at a level of the Oversoul. All the aspects of an Oversoul operate on several levels, several dimensions, simultaneously.

Once I learned to communicate with my soul, and to be brave enough to follow the soul's suggestions, my life changed dramatically. I'm not saying it got easier; if anything, it became more complex and difficult, but at least I finally knew I was moving in the right direction. It has been for me as if the spiritual journey is like a treasure hunt; one clue leading to the next. It took me a long time to quit demanding of the soul to know more than the next single thing. I spent years wanting to know the whole story, the future and the past. I am now a little wiser and realize if the soul had not been so gracious as to keep some things from me, I would have been too scared and intimidated to get from one day to the next, from one clue to the next. I've been scared and often puzzled, elated, surprised, overwhelmed, even; but I remain very, very grateful that my soul is willing to communicate with me and tolerate my resistance and my insistence with humor. The spiritual journey is not about doing a lot, doing it quickly and proving you are bet-ter-taller-faster-smarter-more-attractive than someone else. It is about remembering the truth of who you are and letting the soul be in charge of the ego, letting the soul's suggestions lead the ego into submission to the soul. It is about becoming a soul-infused personality.

Listening to our souls and being brave enough to follow the suggestions, the intuition the soul offers, takes focus, intention, bravery, courage and strength. When we do it, or when I've done it, I've had to give up caring what other people think of me. I've lost friendships, family, the good opinion of people who thought they were in control of me and membership in organi-zations that, at the time, were important to me. I've gone way beyond what other people have thought was right and good for me. Once you have the connection to your soul in a conscious way, it is my experience the opinions of others becomes less important; not completely unimportant, because I would still like to have been able to keep some of the friends. However, I did learn letting go was less costly to me than trying to hold on to people and organizations that feared and judged what was happening to me and judged what I was learning as evil, scary and inappropriate.

The soul whispers. It does not shout. It does not demand. It whispers and it suggests. Learning to know the preferences of the soul can be cul-tivated through intention, prayer and meditation. The most important thing I think we can develop is awareness. If we become aware that we are an immortal soul inhabiting a Human body by choice, we can remove a lot of our fears, especially the fear of death. If we can become aware of the idea the soul created the body for its use, we can remember we are not the body and the body belongs to the soul, not to our ego.

It is my experience; all Humans have a desire to belong to a group, a family, an organization or at least to another person. Without this sense of belonging, the Human always feels vulnerable. Once we make the conscious soul connection, we understand we do belong to the soul and the soul belongs to us. At that point, our vulnerability and our need to belong to others or to organizations usually diminish, or at least it has for me. The sense of loneliness I always felt, even when I was with other people, has subsided. I now am truly never alone. My soul and I are consciously one thing.

I firmly believe every person has the capacity to know their soul in a conscious way. In the beginning, I had fear of knowing. I was afraid of what my soul would demand of me. I had fear of knowing the future. It took actual contact with my soul to alleviate these fears. Having conscious soul contact is the only way I have found to attain peace. Without it, I was always in a state of wondering and a state of trying to live up to my perceived expectations of others. Once I made contact with my soul I also made contact with other spiritual dimensions and became consciously aware that this is certainly not the only reality.

There are many diverse ways people use to communicate with God or their souls; for me, it took meditation. I now always seal the room in which I'm meditating by sealing the room in each direction, as well as above and below me, from any negative influence. In the beginning I meditated by sitting quietly with intention and pencil and paper on my lap to receive guidance. I would take a deep breath, hold the breath and count to myself 111 and exhale. I would take another deep breath, hold the breath and count to myself 222 and exhale. I would take a third deep breath, hold the breath and count to myself 333 and exhale. I would then breathe normally and count backwards from 10 to one and then sit quietly and wait for a response from my soul. The first time I tried this meditation, I received seven pages of writing. Apparently my soul had been waiting for me to be ready to communicate.

I now live with the intention to be available to my soul at all times. I seldom go into a deliberate meditation unless I'm feeling unsure or meditating with a group. This method doesn't work for everyone. There are as many ways to meditate as there are people.

Declaring ourselves to be spiritual, rather than religious, requires a different commitment to the soul. With religion, a person can be religious part of the time and secular part of the time. To be truly spiritual takes a 24/7 commitment to the soul and a willingness to pay attention and follow the intuition of the soul. To a truly spiritual person, there is no separation between their spiritual life and their business, their friendships, their career, their family, their nationality, their commitment to the Earth and Humanity. All of their life becomes spiritually directed from the level of their souls. This does not mean, however, that the entire struggle is over. We learn through struggle.

We do not see the World as it is. We see the World as we are.

Cultivating our spirituality means we become:
What we image.
Reflections of the expressions we use.
An embodiment of the thoughts we project.
An expression of our feelings.
Manifestation of the images we nourish.
A walking demonstration of how we smile.
A personification of how we greet people.
What we focus on most of the time.
A mirror image of our energy patterns.
What we value and intend.
The personality we adopt in dealing with challenges.
The identity we nurture in our mind's eye.
What we affirm and celebrate.

What we think, image, feel, and do—we become
—to our obvious regret or enhancement.

We are here to experience the power of the Divine within us. That gives us the power to create and recreate our lives. We are here as divine representatives to experience our divinity within Human context. We are here to experience eternity in the everyday by learning to live freely—and creatively—in the moment.

If we can truly believe we are souls and are part of God, then it would be helpful to remind ourselves to trust that the soul will not mislead or deprive us. Nor will it allow us to forego learning the lessons we agreed to in our contracts. How we choose to learn them is up to us. We can learn through struggle and pain or we can learn through awareness, intention and joy. The choice is always up to us.

We are often at our best as Humans when faced with tragedy. A disaster occurs: there's a hurricane, tsunami, tornado, earthquake, the twin towers collapse. People are killed, homes destroyed, community and individual lives disrupted, property losses in the billions of dollars. Earthly tragedies cannot be denied. The Hierarchy and our souls have witnessed when disaster strikes, people are stirred to come together, help one another, pray as one and rebuild communities. Often it takes a major loss or threat to activate the best in Humanity. Often it takes a major personal loss for a person to wake up to the fact that they are a soul and part of a much larger organism—GOD.

Let's remember to pray first—instead of as a last resort, and to expect miracles.

5.

Belief, Faith, Knowingness

We can know something because we have read it or heard it from our elders. Most of our beliefs have been handed down to us from others. Some of these people we have considered to be authorities and we've taken their word for what is true without checking it out for ourselves. When we first start questioning, if we ever do, we begin to wonder: Who am I really? Am I what other people have told me? Am I the roles I play?

We are not our names. We are not our bodies. We are not our minds. We are not our occupations. We are not our relationships. We are not our country, race or religion. We are the intangible, invisible, indestructible spiritual Self having these experiences. We are consciousness.

I learned this lesson in 1979. I lost all the roles I was playing up to that point in a nine month period. I found myself in a strange place, alone and without any roles. I sat with a legal pad on my lap and I tried to figure out who I was without a husband, parents, lover, children, a job, friends, family or even being a member of the Episcopal Church. I wrote I AM, and in the space after that I just couldn't seem to figure out what I was without the roles I was used to playing. I did wonder, since I was no longer playing roles, who was inside me even asking this question? I ended up with a whole column of I AM. Of course, at the time, I didn't know that was the answer; that before and after everything else, we are the I AM, the spirit having the Human experience. I didn't understand or learn this for another three years until I began to have direct communication with my soul.

Wayne Dyer in his book, *Your Sacred Self*, says there are ten most common and difficult-to-undo beliefs we have been taught in Western civilization.

MORE IS BETTER – This belief locks us into striving and never really arriving or enjoying life.

To undo this belief, it is important to simplify our lives and to look at what we are attempting to fill within ourselves by striving to have more and more and more.

EXTERNALS ARE TO BLAME FOR THE CONDITIONS OF MY LIFE – We are taught to blame the weather, our parents, the culture, politicians, luck and even illness on heredity or the flu season.

To undo this belief and stop blaming, we must eventually accept total responsibility for our thoughts and actions.

IDEALISM CAN'T COEXIST WITH REALISM – We are taught that only what we can see is real. In actuality, nothing is real and nothing is imagined. Everything is perception.

To undo this belief, we will need to learn to rely on our wisdom mind rather than our ordinary judgmental mind. We must learn to trust our intuition rather than what appears to be happening or what other people tell us.

THERE IS ONLY ONE EXISTENCE AND IT IS PHYSICAL – We are brought up to believe we are our bodies and only what is physical is real.

To undo this belief, it is important to develop an awareness of the observer within ourselves, the one observing the actions and thoughts of the physical being. It is useful to make ourselves available to non-physical realities.

WE ARE SEPARATE AND DISTINCT FROM EVERYONE ELSE – Our education emphasizes believing in sensory experiences. These experiences seem to tell us that we are separate, unique, and special and disconnected from each other and the Earth.

We learn from physicists we are all made from the same substance and so is the Earth. We are only separate in our perception. In actuality, everything is made of one unifying substance.

THERE IS AN "US" VERSUS A "THEM" – We live in a civilization that thrives on this concept and labels and divides families, nationalities, races and members of different political and religious beliefs.

In order to overcome this belief, it is useful to begin to think of ourselves as Universal Humans or at least Global Humans, Planetary Citizens, or Earthlings rather than members of a select group.

PETTY TYRANTS SHOULD BE IGNORED – There are bad people in the World and they should be avoided and ignored.

In order to overcome this belief, we must reach a point of being able to witness the spirit within each person. We may not be comfortable with or approve of their behavior, but at their core they are also spiritual beings. We learn from these people how not to be victims. Everything that comes into our lives is for the purpose of teaching us.

GOALS ARE ESSENTIAL FOR SUCCESS – It is important to have goals and to be aware of our purpose, but also to be flexible in our pursuits.

To overcome the belief that we must have goals, and not deviate from their pursuit, it is important to understand our purpose is to seek guidance from our soul to understand our true purpose in being here, which is expansion. Then to follow what we believe is our purpose and our personal goals with enthusiasm and vigor and trust the Universe is willing to assist us to become all we are capable of becoming.

YOU MUST ALWAYS DO YOUR BEST – Your best leaves no room for improvement. It means you have to give 100 per cent at all times. Continually doing your best involves enormous stress and pressure. Usually you are measuring yourself against someone else's standards.

To overcome this belief, it is important to receive guidance and to follow that guidance to the best of our ability and to not compare ourselves or our performance to that of others. It is important, at the level of our souls, we not be competitive, but that we be creative.

DREAMS ARE NOT REALITY – We are taught there are two separate realities. One is our waking reality; the other is our dream reality.

To overcome this belief, we would do well to understand our dreams and our waking reality are created by the same brain and that these separate energy experiences are interrelated. Again, the most important thing is to cultivate the witness within ourselves that watches both realities.

We are all enrolled in the school of Earth. We chose much of our curriculum before we chose to embody for this incarnation. Blaming what is happening with us on something outside ourselves doesn't serve our spiritual growth.

Beliefs are handed to us. Knowing comes from within. No one can hand you knowing. You can believe a thing, but still have doubt; once you have the experience that proves or disproves the belief, and then you can have knowing. When you have direct experience in your own life, it is easier to give up doubt.

I had believed in Jesus on the word of religious authorities, but doubted much of what was written in the Bible. On two separate occasions in my life, the Master Jesus has materialized in front of me and we have had direct conversations. This definitely moved believing in Him and knowing Him into my reality. I could still doubt myself if I chose and dismiss these experiences as my imagination, but once the knowingness is instilled within me as experience I don't choose to doubt.

I had no belief in the Spiritual Hierarchy, as I'd never heard of them within the context of my Christian education, but, again, when the Masters began to appear to me and converse with me to explain the workings of the Universe, even though I argued I didn't think running the Universe as a corporation was a good idea, I became more than a believer. I now know how the Universe and galaxy operate and what positions are held by what Masters.

I had no belief in extraterrestrials, nor did I desire one, until the Federation brought ships in for me to see them and began their telepathic communication with me to explain my role in the Federation. I am a person who needs personal experience to support what I think I know. I am not a person who is able to operate with blind faith as was encouraged when I was in the Christian churches.

Now I've developed my ability to know, through direct communication, I still depend on my intuition. Intuition is something we all have. Many people are afraid to trust their intuition and will even deny having it. Agreeing to have knowingness is a big step in our spiritual growth because it removes our excuses. Once we have knowingness, we can no longer pretend not to know or honestly use the terms, "Well, I just don't know" or "I'm so confused." I don't personally see the value in believing things just because someone wrote them down or puts them in a newspaper or on TV. I think our most valuable asset as spiritual beings is the spiritual gift of discernment.

I have found it much easier to have faith once I began to demand proof of the Universe. The Universe, our souls, the Masters are all a part of a much larger consciousness. We all have the ability to communicate with this consciousness. What stops us, fear or feelings of unworthiness?

Once we shut down our inner chatter and go into silence we will find our witness, our soul, our God Self, whatever you want to call it. Our first step is to begin to witness our thoughts, then to look at who is witnessing the thoughts and then to follow that part of us, which is our soul. The soul does not make demands. It makes suggestions. We always have the free will to argue, disagree or make conditions under which we will do what the soul suggests. We are not pawns. We are here to be co-creators with our souls.

Self-realization is the only authentic freedom. Authentic freedom knows who you are, why you are here, your purpose in life and where you are going when you leave here. It is knowing your identity is not located in the physical World but in the eternal, changeless World of God. Authentic freedom comes from knowing, not from belief.

We can only have higher awareness by asking for it and seeking it through silence. Many people are afraid of silence. They are afraid of what the soul will ask of them. Higher awareness demands a new agreement with reality. We can doubt or we can ask and listen. We can make an effort to shut down our inner dialogue, the babblings of our ego, and listen to the voice of our soul. We can cultivate the witness. Allowing the higher self to surface as the dominant force in our lives will bring the only lasting peace. Doing this, we can know God on an experiential level.

The first few times I meditated with the intention and desire to hear God, I was not able to shut down my ego thoughts, but I was determined. I listened to what the ego was saying, "This is the dumbest thing you've ever done, this is not going to work, who are you to think God would speak to you, for God's sake, put the phone on the hook, and for God's sake go get a job." I just kept sitting there with the willingness and intention to hear God and suddenly on the right side of my brain there were other words, other than the ranting of my ego. One did not shut up when the other began to impress words into my mind. There was never a voice. It was always just words. I wrote the words and later went back and read the words. I must admit I was expecting a voice. I later learned seeing is of the vibration of the Third and Fourth dimension; hearing is of the Third, Fourth and Fifth dimension; and above that, energetically, there is knowingness. My soul had not agreed to let me see or hear as I had previously requested. They were waiting for me to agree to have knowingness.

Most of the people who are awake at this time came to Earth from higher vibrations than seeing and hearing. If you haven't been able to hear or see spiritually, I invite you to agree to "know", to ask your soul for knowingness. Your soul would not want you to reduce your vibration lower than the one you came in with. That would be like letting you go back to kindergarten. Start where you are now, without fear of what you will be given. You can always argue, refuse or make conditions under which you will attempt what the soul is suggesting. These conditions need to be in writing, because we are operating in the Fourth dimension now, and the rules of the Fourth dimension demand, to have a contract with our soul that allows the soul to intervene on our behalf, we must put our desires in writing.

Don't take what I've said as your belief; try it for yourself. From your own experience, you will develop faith based on your own knowingness and experience rather than following someone else's beliefs. I can assure you higher awareness demands a new agreement with reality, but it also brings peace and serenity.

Every belief you chose to call your own was the best option you had available to you at the time. You are always free to choose again.

6.

Selfishness vs. Selflessness

To develop ourselves and grow spiritually in a healthy way, it is important to practice rational selfishness and rational selflessness. The concepts of selfishness vs. selflessness are central to all religious and mystical philosophies. Romantic love and parenting are normally dependent upon selflessness. In most doctrines, to be good Christians means to be selfless. To be out of balance, in either direction; too selfish (thinking only of ourselves) or too selfless (thinking only of others) for long periods of time is immature, destructive and will lead to irrational behavior.

The moral purpose of all Human life is rational happiness.

Negative emotions are reliable warning signals that a person is acting contrary to one's nature, well-being and happiness. Everyone has the ability to choose what emotions they wish to feel. Happiness, pleasure, and love can only be experienced through emotions. To the extent a person represses emotions, is the extent the person denies that part of reality needed to experience earned pleasures and happiness - which is the moral purpose of Human life.

Repression of emotions is the attempt to deny emotions. Such repression is harmful and entirely different from the suppression of emotions, which can be a valuable, necessary process. Suppression of emotions is an act of discipline in consciously putting aside emotions to experience them later at a more appropriate time or in a more controlled manner. In suppressing an emotion, one is not denying the emotion and remains fully aware of it. Suppression is an important tool for preventing destructive reactions in oneself.

The Human organism must experience emotions in order to psychologically live. If a person continually diminishes self-awareness or represses emotions, that person will steadily lose his or her capacity to feel emotions. To compensate for that deadening of feelings, that person must take increasingly stronger measure to feel something until the only feeling left to feel is pain. The easiest, quickest route to feel pain is through destructive actions.

As a person diminishes his or her awareness and integration capacities, the initiation of longer range, positive actions becomes increasingly difficult. The person will succumb to selecting more and more destructive actions in order to feel something. Destructive actions taken to feel something include manipulating others, lying, initiating force to control or use others, using drugs or alcohol, promiscuity, stealing, injurious masochism or sadism, vandalism, thrill killing, mass murder, waging war, genocide.

Emotions are a real part of every person and, therefore, are part of reality. To know and deal with an undistorted reality, a person must first know one's self, which includes knowing one's own emotions. A person must learn to be aware of feelings in order to prevent destructive emotional reactions. A person must also know one's own emotions in order to effectively share them in a love relationship. Emotions are not subject to condemnation, guilt, or right or wrong judgments...only actions are right or wrong. While everyone innocently experiences negative, irrational emotions, no one ever has to act on such emotions. Since only Human actions are subject to choice, only Human actions (not emotions) are subject to moral judgment. An individual is, however, always responsible for his or her actions. Even if the action is an accident or honest error, one remains responsible for every action.

We need to always think of ourselves first before undertaking any activity or commitment. One of my greatest lessons has been to learn to ask my soul "Is this mine to do?" Before I learned this I would make snap judgments based on what I saw as a need in the other person or situation, something I knew I was capable of doing or fulfilling and I would automatically volunteer without asking my soul the important question, "Is this mine to do?" Invariably, over and over, I would find myself overextended energetically and become resentful and irritable with others. I always felt if it was in front of me it was mine to do. I ended up with roommates who used my things inappropriately, stole from me or were closet alcoholics. I found myself on committees that were impossible to coordinate. I found myself with no time left for myself, no time left for introspection. I filled every hour of every day fulfilling the needs and desires of others. I was a people pleaser. Myself worth came from others; therefore, it could be given or taken away by others. When we don't understand who we are, vehicles the soul has created in order to have access to life on Earth, we tend to believe we are our roles. Once we become clear about who we really are, vehicles through which the soul, God, can operate in this dimension, we can see more clearly what roles the soul wishes to play and what activities in which the soul wishes to engage.

A person must be very selective to protect their own time; otherwise, others will waste your time at every opportunity by drawing you in to listen to their problems or demanding you help them with their work or projects. Many people will attempt to guilt you into helping them with things they would be better off doing alone. Often they will draw you into their scenario and then later blame you for not doing more to help or expect you to become responsible for the result of their lives. It is important not to enable others to remain weak. Always ask, "Is this mine to do?"

Spiritual maturity, sanity, happiness and health are all dependent on what I call "rational selfishness." We have a responsibility to think of our own health, our own time and our own desires first. Once we've done this, we can make conscious decisions to choose to sacrifice our time and our desires in favor of selfless activity. If we always think of others first, and allow our time and energy to be used up by others, we have nothing left for our own desires and happiness. If we make helping others into what we trick ourselves into thinking will keep them near us, indebted to us, make them love us, make them respect us, we will be sadly mistaken.

People who do not save some of themselves for themselves and make taking care of others 100% of their life are not accomplishing what they came to Earth to experience. It is a way of abdicating our lives to someone else or others in general. It is a way of escaping what we came to do. Rational selfishness depends on thinking of yourself first, your own health, and your own satisfaction with your life. If you spend all your energy on others, whether you admit it or not, you will eventually resent the people you are helping and resentment breeds ill health.

In relationships it is important for there not to be just one giver and one taker. It is important, even in the case of children, that there is an energy exchange between people, even people who are too young to physically reciprocate to those who give to them. If a young mother is left to take care of small children 100% of the time without relief or help from others, they will begin to feel used and resentful. They may not admit this, because that would obviously make them "bad mothers", and they may deny this, but the feelings will be buried deep within their subconscious. They may nag, gossip, overeat, withdraw affection or lash out and punish the children or other people inappropriately.

Many relationships depend on each individual playing certain roles for the other. Traditionally, the female is the care giver and the male the bread winner. Even in same sex relationships roles are usually defined or decided upon by one person being more of the care giver to the other. There is nothing wrong with being a care giver, but to be healthy one must receive care.

We are responsible for caring for ourselves first before we give to others. If we do not, we do not have anything extra to give and we are giving from our essential self. We are responsible for protecting our essential self energy for use by our own bodies and lives. To attract or maintain relationships that use up our time and energy, leaving none with which to pursue our goals, is against spiritual law. If you have friends or family who phone you and talk and talk and talk about their problems or the problems of the World, drop them, don't answer the phone. For this purpose God gave us caller ID.

In the case of relationships and friendships, it is important both parties are givers and receivers. In many cases, relationships are unequal energetically. If a male has not discovered how to access his own feminine energy, he will constantly need to be in the presence of females to use their energy to fulfill this need. If a female has not developed her ability to access her own male energy, she will always need to be in close relationships with men. This may be accomplished by being "daddy's girl." Or it may be accomplished by always being married or having multiple suitors.

Men who need female energy may be unhealthily tied to their mothers or may need multiple sex partners. Men often only know how to fulfill this feminine energy need through sex. Women learn early on how to gain male attention in order to fulfill this need in themselves.

In ongoing relationships, if one partner is not giving the caring the other person desires, it is common for them to cause an argument or disagreement. Arguments raise the level of energy, though not in a positive way. If a male can cause a woman to feel fear or anger he can then drain her energy. If a female does not feel as if her friend or partner is paying attention to her she may often cause an argument to get that person's attention and energy. Once she has gotten the other person "worked up" she can drain that person's energy. This is the reason many couples fight and then make up through having sex in order to get the energy fix they can't produce for themselves.

As long as a friend or partner can engage you in an argument, especially an irrational argument, they can steal your energy. One of the steps in spiritual maturity and energy health is to learn to refuse to participate in irrational arguments. If you refuse to participate, refuse to get hooked, the other person must eventually seek other ways to fulfill their need or, in the best case scenario, they wake up and face responsibility for their own actions and their own lives. The rational person will remain healthy, projecting their desires into their own lives and following what is to their best interests.

It is a banner day when we finally wake up to the fact, we cannot change another person.

When the healthy person walks away from a potential argument, the other person is left in their own self-made trap. This is especially true when adults are dealing with teenagers. Teenagers have a lot of energy, much of which they do not know how to channel in a positive way. They are eager to pick fights, especially verbal ones, with their peers and especially their parents. They use these confrontations with parents to wear them down energetically to feed off of their energy and to attempt to get their own way. It is the responsibility of the parents to see what is happening energetically with the child and with themselves and to not agree to engage in irrational arguments.

When a person constantly acts against their own self-interest by being selfless and sacrificial, anger builds up inside them. To continue putting others' needs in front of one's own, to continue sacrificing, one must suppress that anger. Suppressed anger is capable of exploding or being repressed to the extent it turns into an illness. Even sweet little old ladies who have spent their lives sacrificing for others, as the church has taught them, have repressed their true desires and emotions in favor of being "good." Whenever a person denies a part of themselves that is natural and wholesome then the natural drive will be expressed in a distorted and unwholesome way.

I, not unlike many women, turned to religion in an attempt to give more meaning to my life than being a good daughter, wife and mother. The church told me my sacrifices and unhappiness was the right thing to do. They also gained a free volunteer employee for many years while I was stuck in the belief sacrificing my life completely for others was the "holy" thing to do.

Often when people spend their lives primarily serving others they often eventually break and run away because they know no other way to change their circumstances. This is often referred to as a mid-life crisis. A man may suddenly realize he has spent all his time providing for his family and not thinking of his own needs and desires. Of course, there are those who are also emotionally arrested adolescents who have spent their time and money doing as they wished and expected their wives or partners to be the adult. For women, they often wake up one morning and realize they have given their lives away to their parents, their husbands, their children and can't remember who they really are other than the roles they play for other people. I actually thought the roles were who I was until all the roles were removed at once. I sat in a chair with pen and paper and asked myself, "Who am I without the roles?" I would write, "I AM..." over and over, not realizing I was giving myself the answer. Before and after all the roles I play, I am the I AM, God desiring to consciously live through this vehicle.

It is healthy to keep these guidelines in mind when dealing with intimate relationships:

1. Put yourself first.
2. What is best for you is also best for all concerned.
3. We harm those we love the most when we give into their irrationalities.
4. We also contribute to their irrational behavior when we let them get away with it.
5. Those who refuse to grow up have to be put into the position of facing the consequences of their actions.
6. Only when a person accepts responsibility for their actions will they mature and enhance the possibilities for building an increasingly rewarding future with a romantic partner.

Our lives must be lived from a place of balance for us to be emotionally and physically healthy. At times we must act selfishly in order to have time, energy and stamina to then give to others unselfishly. We can have compassion for others without sacrificing ourselves, unrealistically fulfilling the needs and desires of others. When we practice rational selfishness we practice self-respect and we offer that same respect to others.

Most of us were accused, at some time when we were children, of being selfish when we would not share something we had with others. It was used only in a derogatory way. We learn the way to please others is to give up ourselves and what we desire in favor of the desires of others. We live our lives for others rather than for ourselves. In living this way we lose our self-respect. We allow others to tell us what is right and what to believe in order to please them or to fit into a pattern that is not our real selves.

Developing self-respect, if you have not been respected by your parents or partners, can be very challenging. At first, a person can feel guilty and selfish when they pull back from being used and choose to analyze what would really make them happy. If a person doesn't have self-respect, it is fairly easy to spot; especially if they get themselves into a position of authority. They talk down to others and make efforts to intimidate them. They do not have inner feelings of confidence and self-worth; if they did, they would be able to extend that self-respect to others.

Religions, for the most part, foster the idea of humility. It is a false way of developing humility through being selfless. A person who practices rational selfishness, who doesn't latch onto readymade dogmatic answers, develops a true humility in the sense they are willing to acknowledge the mistakes they make in life. They can admit their mistakes because they have a solid base of self-esteem and personal confidence. They can acknowledge they don't have all the answers, that they don't know everything. They are willing to keep continually learning throughout their lives.

An individual is solely responsible for their life and choices.

Each individual is solely responsible for his or her own actions. That includes being responsible for what goes in and out of one's own mouth. Mouth responsibility is a very important part of spiritual growth. We need to be responsible for the food, drink, drugs, smoke, genitalia that go into our mouths and the words that come out. Unnatural highs always destructively disintegrate a person's physical or psychological life, or both. The ultimate high, however, comes from feeling in control of one's own self, living honestly, rationally and productively.

Consciousness does not automatically take place. To become conscious, we must become conscious of who we are individually as units of consciousness and then ultimately understand our relationship to the Oneness of all life. If we attempt this from following the dogma set out by someone outside ourselves, we will fail. This process can only be accomplished from a point of self reflection.

To follow a set dogma creates a split in the brain. Dogma is a belief of the intellect and allows the left brain to control thinking and action. Often, after years of following dogma, which leads to irrational selflessness or irrational selfishness, a person's right brain rebels and points out the falseness of the dogma. This point often leads to great confusion. If what I've believed isn't real, isn't true, what am I to believe? There comes a time in most people's lives when intellectualizing is either no longer satisfying or no longer fulfills their true needs. Often this can only come at a point when logic fails us. "When all else fails, turn to God."

7.

Understanding The Self

Every person is unique and imbued with unimaginable spiritual power. Our task is to imagine that power, reach for it, and bring it to light. To do this, we must begin with the self, since we can't give what we don't have, teach what we don't know, or describe where we haven't been. Step one to a better World is to cherish, explore, and understand the self. To be blunt, when I know my own anger, I will more clearly comprehend why somebody else picks up a gun. When I know my own grief, I will have more compassion, definitely not less, for someone who one day just gives up.

Plumbing the depths of our own minds and hearts is an act of spiritual psychology. As we learn more about ourselves we start to make changes within. We ask our anger what it wants from us, what particular fear it's surrounding; then, we can disarm that fear and, with it, the anger. We become more peaceful, centered, balanced, and willing to ask for what we need and desire from life, trusting that somehow we'll get it. We serve the World and other people so much more authentically—and therefore more efficiently when we know them as something more than just the means to meet our emotional needs. The mysterious side of personal and ultimately, global change reveals itself in how amazingly a changed mind can change things. This is because things are merely congealed ideas.

With new mental causes come new material effects.

Contemplation verses action? Doing work in consciousness requires we start with the end in mind. We don't just sit around thinking about ourselves. We envision a happy, peaceful, prosperous World for every single soul, but we can't do this well when our own minds and hearts are in turmoil, so we start there, and keep revisiting the self to see what it's up to, as we're practicing meditation, affirmative prayer and other useful spiritual practices. These actually take up less time than worrying and resenting, we can get busy brightening the area where we are.

Faced with a storm-ravaged community, we imagine it rebuilt and thriving while reaching for a shovel or making food for the people who are manning the shovels. We see the perfect spiritual person within the ill friend as we drive that friend to the doctor. If we look at the enormity and sadness of what is happening in the World we can lose heart, but if we do the thing, in front of us, that needs doing; we can be part of the solution. Step one to a better World is to cherish, explore, and understand the self.

There are as many ways to serve as there are people to do so, more really, because in serving, we uncover countless talents within ourselves we didn't know were there. The gift our personal spiritual journeying brings to the table is a natural, durable, healthy optimism that we're all getting somewhere.

When we encounter situations of slavery we have a responsibility to do what it takes to realize for ourselves we are free and to take that feeling of freedom and imagine it also for others, without too much attachment to what anyone else needs to do about it. When we do this we enlarge our vision of Humankind beyond the labels oppressor and oppressed.

All people are experiences that God is having of Itself at the level of that person. In the relative sense, we may agree there are people who should not be in positions of leadership, or even left at large, due to the danger they pose to others and themselves. Yet in the absolute sense, there are no "bad" people, only people who are oblivious to their own unmet emotional needs, and they are trying to work out their pain on the stage of the World.

This is a different way of seeing and perceiving the World, because we have been taught to mete out praise and condemnation where each is due based on a personal value system. We have prized being right because it requires less effort, especially the mental kind. We are now being asked to perceive things from a higher plane of awareness.

Spirituality is a lot easier to explain than it is to live, as it entails unlearning duality and embracing oneness.

The World is made up of individuals, each of whom inhabits that dimension we call consciousness, and who is, therefore a co-creator with God, and thus able to change his or her own circumstances. To simplify our conversations, we often lump these individuals together into tribes, nations, religions, and so on, and then by applying our own value judgments, we may separate them further into like us or unlike us, safe or threatening, right or wrong, and worthy of love or not. But even in societies where the "personal will" seems utterly submerged beneath a collective ideology, every person still has spiritual power and free will.

Everything we perceive, we relate to previous perceptions. Then, we categorize each piece. This collecting of perceptions we call knowledge. The facility for categorizing them is our understanding. Knowledge plus understanding equals worldly wisdom and expertise about this dimension of life. I longed for a context in which to frame all the information, an anchor of truth that did not change, I found that in the Universal Laws. I came to understand not only is there a system, but also behind all the seeming chaos there is an orderly patterning of intelligence unfolding itself into form through us and through nature.

Pick out one situation in the World you desire to be different than it is. Now, the situation you select will likely have two opposing viewpoints to it, and the tendency is to align yourself with one of them. Now, turn your attention to the situation you're seeking to remedy. What would you put in its place? Focus all your attention on the positive, beneficial opposite of the condition. How would we end war, which is exciting, stimulating, and filled with heroic actions, selfless sacrifices and senses heightened among those in combat? What exactly is peace? Is it the absence of war? That's not compelling enough for us to create it. So the task is to imagine peace as being even more exciting and heroic than armed conflict, because now in the place of two relative sides there is the absolute One expressing Itself. Everyone is together in this energized creative endeavor and passionately involved in co-creating the ongoing common good. We will logically think, well, I'm willing, but others won't cooperate. We may still believe other people are spiritually unreachable, or this new, peaceful place, we're imagining, has past offenders that would skate by without the due punishment for their past actions.

We cannot hold the belief some others don't deserve good and expect to attain it ourselves. Subjective mind, the realm where causes generate effects, can't objectify between us and them, so what we believe about others comes, eventually, to surround us.

Now, pray to know every person on the planet is fully aware that he or she has a choice, and this choice is received and acted upon by the only Power there is. Knowing this for others does not manipulate, coerce or control them. It invites them back to their innocence, wonder, and their "heart knowing." Knowing this for yourself brings you to realize, in the deepest possible sense, in the eyes of the One, there are no others. We are like a drop of water in the vast ocean of water. We are all made from the same stuff, have the same nature, and have the same power. The difference is in degree not essence. We are what we think, what we believe and what we expect.

THE DIFFERENCE BETWEEN EMPATHY AND TRUE SPIRITUAL CONTACT

Spiritual contact is done from the level of the soul, the contact of soul with soul and is not a merging with another person emotionally. We do not lose inward contact with ourselves in order to experience it. It is not an energetic intrusion of one person into another's energetic space. It is an authentic meeting of one individual with another; through soul to soul communication.

Many sensitive people avoid relationships because they tend to feel overwhelmed or feel the need to lose themselves in the other person, to lose touch with their own feelings, thoughts and needs. But relating with other people from one's soul to the other's soul means one maintains inward contact with their own inner self at the same time as one experiences the intimacy of oneness with another person. The rigid defensive boundary between one's self and other people dissolves. The actual boundaries of inward contact become clearer.

BREAKING THE HABIT OF BEING YOURSELF HOW TO LOSE YOUR MIND AND CREATE A NEW ONE

Scientists are beginning to more and more use the terminologies of energy and frequency, the language of mysticism. The science of energy and frequency can help us to reshape our lives, to make them better. Awareness is one thing, but to embody awareness is another thing completely. The frontal lobe—40 percent of the entire brain—gives us the ability to observe ourselves. We can learn what we're feeling, see how we're acting, and give ourselves permission to change. Becoming mindful and conscious of our subconscious self is where change starts.

Our personality creates our personal reality. How we think, act, and feel create our reality. To create a new personal reality, we have to examine how we think and what our beliefs are, look at our emotions and our conditioned emotional responses and change them. Transformation involves reconditioning, and reconditioning is a process. It's not enough to desire change. The process of change requires an unlearning process as well as a learning process. We have to prune some old synaptic connections. Insight never changes behavior. For example understanding what caused a panic attack won't resolve the anxiety. Knowing the cause of the reaction won't change it, only changing our thinking can change the neo-cortex. We cannot make a quantum leap from our habitual thoughts to new behavior without changing our thoughts. Quantum leaps always involve discontinuing current behavior, meaning we have to be willing to jump from where we are into a whole new (and unfamiliar) vibrational experience and that's rarely comfortable.

We're conditioned to think if something is uncomfortable something is wrong. We live in a culture striving to maintain a certain feeling of good, and when we are uncomfortable, we look outside ourselves to make it go away. That's when we become addicted to something outside of us. But the real answer is inside, and we can access it there. The only way we can begin to actually create change in our lives is to become conscious of our unconscious thoughts and beliefs and change them to agree with the change we desire. Unfortunately we often wait until we are experiencing trauma before we look that deeply into ourselves.

Manifestation requires we get clear about what we desire and then change our actions to align with our intentions to create new experiences which create new emotions. The moment we have a new emotional experience, we feel it. The chemicals get created in the emotional brain. We need to teach the body emotionally what we understand intellectually. Breaking the habit of being our usual selves requires embodying new beliefs, which involves teaching the body new ways of being by using the chemical reactions in the brain. We have to change our focus because when we focus on past experiences, we are actually reinforcing those old neuro pathways in the brain, which releases the same old chemical mix, causing the body to relive it all and reinforce the habit. **We can't go into a new future by holding on to the feelings of the past.** When we let go of the emotions connected to the past, we can begin to see the new landscape, new possibilities, but we need to get it into the body for it to take hold.

Effecting change is not a onetime event. It's a layered process because the body has been highly trained for years to serve one's thoughts, and there are strong chemical associations in place. As we shift one emotion, the body will default to the next line. Layer by layer, we need to confront those. We are reminding ourselves of who we don't want to be, we have to repeatedly remind ourselves who we really are, as aspects of God, and how we desire to be.

To create a new future for ourselves we need to have criteria and ideas about it, then lay out a clear intention, rehearse it mentally, get in touch with the feeling, and teach our body to recognize the experience before it happens. After we do the work of raising our vibration, getting clear, writing it down and releasing it we need to leave the out-workings to the quantum field. We have the ability to transcend a low vibration by adopting thoughts aligned with Universal Truth and training our bodies to understand the new emotional experience.

It requires we stay conscious, refrain from reliving the past, use meditation to activate the feeling of that which we desire, and then let go, allowing our expectations and actions to align with our desires and intentions—all the while inviting the Universe to surprise us. We live in the same vibration we create in; what we attract will match our vibration. From a brain-chemistry perspective, cultivating gratitude also contributes to rewiring the brain and retraining the body. If we couple our body-feeling of gratitude with an event your mind conjured up, our body begins to believe emotionally and chemically the event has already occurred. We don't need a reason to be grateful.

No matter what the lips may be saying, the inner thought out-speaks them, and the unspoken word often carries more weight than the spoken.
Dr. Ernest Holmes

The Universe in which we live is intelligent and constantly responding to our thoughts and feelings. To the extent we learn to control these mental states we control our environment and experiences. Mind and matter are unquestionably related. The principles can be applied not only to your body, but to all aspects of life.   Take a moment to notice what within you is stirring. Then, activate your divine imagination. What shape do you want your life to take? The choice is yours.

UNITY AND DIVERSITY

The dazzling display of diversity in this Universe is the very thing that points to an underlying Unity. There could be no form without the ongoing animating presence of the Formless. We have a spiritual calling to be aware of our unity while delighting in our diversity.

Mystics say when we have broken with the God of tradition and given up belief in the God of rhetoric, the Creator God can fire our hearts with Its Presence. Even scientists are now realizing our link to the Unlimited Creative Intelligence is through our minds.

We as a species are so angry and violent because we have lost sight of our true Self. The God we invented has not kept us from war and hatred. Talking about loving God is meaningless if we do not also love Humanity. Admonishments to resist temptation do not cure addiction in the way a raised awareness of one's own worth does. A claim of Human dominion over the Earth is dangerous unless we feel the unity and interdependence of all life. Dominion is the name of a level of Angelic life we were to emulate. It did not mean we were to dominate, use and abuse the Earth and its creatures.

We are all one in the field of pure intelligence and love. The Creative Process is constant and must individualize itself. It is active in each one of us. The more we sense our unity with It, with intelligence and love and with each other, the more our lives can function in a smooth and natural flow of peace, love, abundance, vitality, and creativity.

How we perceive what is happening gives meaning to our experience. If we look a problem in the face and declare, "This is nothing but a temporary manifestation of old ideas and has no power to reproduce itself without my participation," then we are operating from our power center. This is how we prove the presence of the Higher Power firsthand. God does not intervene. To do so would be to disallow individuality. God, as the Law of Co-creation, responds to the meaning we give to the moment.

As we practice the creative process of giving expression to that which we desire to see in our lives and watching it increase; we prove the Law. It is when we claim our whole self, as a personification of the same consciousness that is giving rise to the Universe; we see the results we desire.

God does not withhold forgiveness, or deny us the right to live as we choose. Living spiritually is simple, but not easy, because it requires we live without making excuses, without pointing fingers, without holding onto resentments, without denying possibility in any situation, or declaring anything or anyone to be irreparable. Spirituality is an infinite and completely renewable resource; it can be tapped forever and will never be exhausted. Spirituality is about choosing principled responses—first in thought and then in action—regardless of the material, emotional, or physical outcome. Spirituality is not weak, impractical, or superfluous; it is a real force for personal and social change.

Gandhi, Dr, Martin Luther King Jr., Rosa Parks and others like them were operating from the Law of Attraction and the Law of Mental Equivalency, whether stated or not. They embodied the spirit of reconciliation, unity and justice because that is what they intended to achieve. They become the change they were seeking, which was not an easy path.

We are the Earthly representatives of Universal Intelligence. Somewhere in us, there is a means to value the whole of ourselves, and we need to find the means of integrating all of it.

If we do not quiet our minds and our lives, the turbulent waters present within them will never reflect the true image of who we are. It is the Oneness that happens only when our intellect is still and we are then able to connect with the Creator Consciousness of Infinite Mind and God's love. When one eliminates only intellect thinking and words, the truth becomes apparent. The still pond is a metaphor for entering the one Mind.

"There is an Infinite Mind from which all things come. The Mind is through, in and around Humans."
Dr. Ernest Holmes

When we can love the unlovable and forgive the unforgivable we are free.

The Cosmic Christ Consciousness resides within each of us and it waits upon our conscious cooperation with it.

We are not Human beings seeking a spiritual experience; we are spiritual beings immersed in a Human experience. We have a responsibility to have mystic communication even in the midst of daily common affairs.

8.

Resistance

When I ask some people to write down their desires they tell me they don't know what they desire or they don't have any desires. I've always found this easy to believe from my own experience, in the beginning. I've found if we don't know what we desire, a hidden resistance, in our subconscious is making us hesitate to find our true heart's desires. My subconscious beliefs were keeping me from being aware of my true heart's desires.

Reasons for resistance hide in our subconscious. Positive thinking alone will not take us past the buried obstacles in our subconscious. We have to find the source of the resistance before we can move past it. Our resistance will stay dormant as long as we are not threatening it by trying something new.

When we start moving toward a goal we really feel we desire our resistance will leap out of hiding and start trying to convince us to stay as we are, to not risk, changing is dangerous, we can't be sure of success, we don't have enough information to proceed, we don't have a degree in that area, we don't have enough money to begin, we're not smart enough, we can't make a living doing what we desire. Our resistance will stay dormant as long as we are not threatening it by attempting something new, something challenging. It will throw out all kinds of objections: "What are you doing?" "You're going to get in trouble." "This isn't for you." "This is a stupid idea." "You don't know how to do this." "Who do you think you are?" "You are going to fail." "You're going to make a fool of yourself." "You are going to be disappointed." "You're going to end up homeless and be a bag lady."

Our resistance, our ego, is trying to protect us from danger and from learning about Spirit. When we start to act toward accomplishing a desire the ego considers dangerous it will start trying to block our path by making us feel guilty, or ashamed, or inadequate, or hopeless. We need to pay attention to these messages that come up when we start to move in a new direction. "What about your parents? "If you are too good at this everyone will hate you." "If you're successful you will never find a husband." "But you were supposed to be a lawyer, a doctor, a banker; something that will make you a living." "You were supposed to get married and let someone else take care of you." "You should not exceed what your father has done. You'll make him feel bad." "Your brother told you you're not smart, and that's true." "You know they don't call them starving artists shows for nothing." "How could you possibly think you can make a living doing something like that?" We want these messages to come to our awareness so we can design a strategy to beat them.

There is a great deal of difference between having a job, having a career, having work, and having a calling or a mission. Often we only think of ministers as having a calling, but truthfully we all have something our soul is calling us to do. We need to have life work that feels worth doing. To have a job with no meaning doesn't feed our soul. Unfortunately inside most of us is the feeling truly meaningful work has to be on a giant scale, or has to lead to a kind of worldly "greatness," like an Olympic medal or at least a national or worldwide recognition of some sort. Check your own thoughts when you ask yourself, "What do I think meaningful work would mean to me?" "What makes work really worthy?"

Every time we worry we could get trapped in some kind of work we don't care about, we're dealing with the problem of meaningfulness. Usually in the back of our minds is the thought somehow we have to make a contribution to something, be acknowledged, and do something that matters or we're just fooling around.

The ego is focused on survival. The soul is focused on thriving. Most of us think about work as a way to finance our lifestyle rather than a way to satisfy our soul's desires, our heart's desires. Forget whatever you were taught about "meaningful work" and begin to notice what around you catches your attention. Awareness of what actually interests you holds the key to what is meaningful to you. When you're doing your "right" work you will feel connected, both to your soul and to the World outside you.

The first step to finding work that fits us is to understand the connection between doing what we love and doing something worth doing, something that has meaning, because they are one and the same thing. When something really matters to us, we must bring it into our lives. Without an activity that really matters to us, we're going to feel empty.

When we are doing work we love it's a gift to the World as well as feeding our soul.

We do not have to choose between pleasing ourselves and doing something meaningful. If you try to do what our parents and society say is right for us rather than what we feel is right, usually we won't feel satisfied or fulfilled. We are not obligated to fulfill the desires of other people. We are obligated to fulfill the desires of our soul.

Our souls created our bodies in order to have vehicles in this dimension through which to accomplish certain goals for the soul, the Earth and Humanity. Our egos took over the bodies and they try to convince us we are the body. The ego's job is to keep the body safe, to keep the body alive. It attempts to do this by causing us to fear change. Once we remember we are not our bodies; we are souls inhabiting bodies our lives can be different. We have a mission. The soul sent us. The soul has an agenda. Once we remember this and agree to communicate with the soul we can begin to remember the mission.

I was a banker, because my Father thought I should be. Back then banks closed at 3:00 o'clock and to him it was the perfect profession for me. I could work and still be home to fix dinner for my husband and be home for my children when they came home from school. At the time I took on this profession I had neither children nor a husband. It was an O.K. job, but it wasn't exciting and it wasn't fulfilling. I always felt there had to be more, but I didn't feel I was qualified to do anything else, since I had not gone to college.

Years later, when I finally turned my life back over to the soul and began to have soul communication through knowingness and intuition, the soul explained the mission was for me to be an artist, a writer, a spiritual teacher and counselor. I didn't feel smart enough, well educated enough for any of this, so I argued for my limitations. I had tremendous resistance to thinking of myself as an artist. I had no known talent and no art education. I didn't have a degree in art or education. How could I be a teacher? The soul assured me I wasn't the one going to do the art or the teaching or the writing. My job was to be willing to allow the soul to do these things through me; my job was to show up and to surrender to the soul. One of the words I've never liked is surrender, the others are discipline, and frugal. To be a writer I would have to be disciplined. To be an artist, since they were called "starving artist shows" I would likely have to live frugally. None of this sounded appealing to be. My body and my mind had tremendous resistance.

Sometimes we as Humans have to reach bottom before we are willing to surrender. In 1982 I had reached a level of depression that made me willing to surrender. I had a hundred and five dollars in the World and no job. I gave up. I turned my life over to God. I agreed I would do anything, say anything, go anywhere God wanted me to go, if God would talk to me. I expected God to sound like Charlton Hesston, but He didn't. Instead I began to be led by my soul through meditation, books falling off shelves, and strong knowingness and intuition to attempt to paint in watercolor. I amazed myself. Spirit, through me, turned me into an artist, a writer, a spiritual teacher and counselor. I've had resistance every step of the way.

Each time a new challenge was expected of me I hesitated. When the soul suggested I sell all my belongings and begin to travel in my car with only what would fit in my car, my ego went nuts. I thought of a million reasons why I couldn't support myself on the road as a homeless person, but I did it for years and as long as I followed the knowingness, the intuition everything worked out. My ego thought my traveling alone was insane. I had to work hard to listen beyond what the ego would throw at me every day. I had tremendous resistance to not having a home, but I was always taken in by lovely people.

When the soul wanted to start doing spiritual counseling through me; at first I resisted, then I gave in, but I censored what the soul wanted to say, because my ego was invested in my being accurate. When the soul would suggest to me to tell the person it would be useful for their soul, for them to take a trip to Santa Fe, N.M. during September 23-25th, I would restructure the message and say something like, "Have you ever considered taking a trip to the Southwest?" I resisted giving specifics, like dates and the actual names of people and places, because I didn't want to give them anything they could later say wasn't accurate or didn't happen when I had indicated. After a short time, the soul pointed out I was cheating these people. I had a tremendous reaction to the word "cheating" and told the soul I didn't understand what the soul meant. "You're not giving them the full informa-tion available to you. You're afraid you can be proven to be inaccurate. Your ego wants to be right." Once again I had to surrender.

When the soul wanted to start toning through my body, I had tremen-dous resistance. What will people think? I don't even know how to sing. How can I tone correctly if I don't know anything about music? When the soul wanted to have me get down on my knees in front of the client and tone into their knees to release the spiritual secrets they had brought with them; I balked. When I learned doing so brought the information from their knees into their conscious mind, I gave in. When the soul decided it was important to allow my soul to speak prior to Earth languages through my body; I resisted. Then I gave up and allowed it to happen. When the soul wanted to begin to channel through the body to teach, I studied and made notes on 3x5 cards and thought, I can do this. I would prepare and then never get to the event with the cards. I had to finally give up my resistance and let the soul do the teaching. I learned if I took four deep breaths when I got in front of the audience to ground myself, open my heart to my soul, connect to my higher self and to connect to the higher selves of the audience the words that were needed for the audience to hear would come through me from their souls into my soul and out of my mouth.

Each time the soul wanted to do a new thing through my body; I resisted. I feared looking foolish. I feared being homeless. I feared not being able to take care of myself physically and financially. But the soul always came through as soon as I surrendered to the new mission, the new talent, the new event.

I got used to traveling in the United States and driving myself around. When the soul began to want me to call people I'd never met, and asked to meet with them to deliver messages from their soul; I resisted. "These people are going to think I'm nuts, that I'm some sort of kook," I thought. I surrendered and made the calls. Some people would hang up. Some people would need to meet me at the Denny's to check me out before they would take me home with them. My favorite people would respond with, "I asked for a channel three weeks ago what took you so long to get here?"

When the soul suggested they wanted me to travel to the middle of the Amazon jungle of Peru, you can bet your life I resisted. I'm not your jungle kind of girl. By this time I had finally figured out that the messages coming from my soul were not orders; they were suggestions and I had a right to resist, hesitate, argue, or make conditions under which I could do what was being suggested. I made a long list of conditions under which I could go to Peru. It took the soul two weeks to fulfill all of my conditions and I surrendered and went to Peru.

I haven't given up my resistance, but I have learned the soul does know more than I do and my soul can be trusted to come through for me. I am clear there is more to me than my body and this body belongs to my soul. I'm not sure if all the resistance my ego has to letting the soul use the body as it chooses will ever go away, but it has certainly diminished through the years. It hasn't stopped me from reacting with, "You want me to do what!" each time a new assignment is suggested.

Almost yearly my soul would suggest, "You must surrender more." This message would make me furious at first, because I would think the soul meant something physical. I had already relinquished my positions in the church, the community I grew up in, my husband, my parents, my children, my home, my profession and what I had previously thought of as my security. Later I would realize the soul meant, "give up that belief, that fear, that doubt, that attitude, that resistance, and not something physical."

OUR RESISTANCE TO BEING ALL WE CAN BE IS ALWAYS BASED ON FEAR.

Every experience in life is a lesson nudging us to wake up and to explore our potential. Making sense of the World is not as important as being happy. This World was designed not to make sense, but to foster growth.

God does not choose the qualified.
He qualifies those who choose to serve.

9.

Choosing The 2 by 4 or The Feather Method

"If you can learn from hard knocks,
you can also learn from soft touches."
- Carolyn Kenmore

The truth is, nobody escapes this life without encountering some misfortune. The face of misfortune differs widely in appearance, and when it occurs, it stops us in our tracks, forcing us to take notice of the truth of our lives, or we blame someone else for our misfortune. Often, the misfortunes of others seem obvious. We see clearly what they should have done to change their lives. But when the misfortune happens to us, and we are in the midst of it, life seems to be presenting us with a series of cryptic messages. The truth is there have been previous feather messages, which we previously avoided and now we are experiencing the result of a 2 by 4 message. If we ignore the 2 by 4 event as a message the next step will be a brick wall, which will stop us in our tracks.

You know from your own experience changes normally come about gradually. Usually we hang onto our current situations until we can see the bridge that can take us to the next crossing. We ignore the whispers, the feather-like touches of Spirit and wait for more clarity; we wait and want to know for sure before we proceed. If we wait too long and postpone change, Spirit has no choice but to create an event to force the change, a 2 by 4 event. When this happens we are often forced to make the change abruptly, abandoning all paths of security and reasonableness. It would help if and when these 2 by 4 events take place we could move into the uncharted territory with trust that we are on the verge of a great personal discovery. But usually we are in shock and scare ourselves to death and/or make ourselves miserable.

Spirit is subtle. Usually our intuition, the still, small voice within, is more like a whisper or the touch of a feather. If we ignore the repetitious touches of the feather, the whispers, the next choice the soul has is to give us the message in a more dramatic way. I call this the 2 by 4 method. Our lives take turns for the worse or the better in proportion to how each one of us fulfills or evades our inner calling to change. In opening ourselves to Spirit's influence, our destiny is fulfilled. We, however, resist and want to know exactly "how" this is going to work out? We use excuses for not following the subtle guidance of Spirit, demanding to hear a voice, most often claiming Spirit doesn't speak to us; we don't hear a voice because Spirit doesn't use a megaphone, Spirit whispers.

If we wait for a burning bush or a big booming voice to point the way or give us proof this is the right direction, we can wait forever. Spirit gives nudges, feather touches. We are expected to listen, to remain conscious. If we insist on ignoring our intuition, the subtle hunches, the lesson will come with more force and seemingly without warning. Accidents may happen to get our attention, if we are ignoring our situation by rushing from one activity to another, never giving ourselves any quiet time to listen to our souls. We may lose the job we are hanging onto, even if we hate it, because we say we don't know what else to do. If we refuse to budge from a relationship, a job, a place we are living and it's spiritually time to move on, we are setting ourselves up for a 2 by 4 experience. I've often tried to ignore my intuition, because it does not compute to my logic.

Often the 2 by 4 comes in the form of the body developing a disease or being involved in an accident. If we need to slow down to listen, the body will give us that opportunity. We create accidents and diseases when our egos are so resistant to change nothing else will stop us. Some lessons are so unique as to only be learned through illness. Especially if we have taken our bodies for granted and pushed ourselves beyond reason. We often prefer to claim ignorance and prefer to think the world has forced this misfortune upon us. Spiritual maturity causes us to begin to ask: "What is this experience trying to teach me?

Anytime we hear, see or feel something three or more times, especially within a short time period, it's information worthy of our attention. These signs give us feedback about our current belief system, since our thoughts attract mirroring experiences. We are to use these signs to heal beliefs that dishonor us and move us in the direction that our guidance points us.

"There is no blame if we miss the sign the first time or the second or the third, but if we continually ignore what we are given to understand, then surely it will be difficult to see the purpose of the next test. Truth is not delivered on a silver platter but is distilled within from hard work and good observation."
– Reshad Field

When a strong creative urge takes us in what appears to be the wrong direction, we have a tendency to believe that urge to be wrong. But oftentimes that urge springs from a positive source – it's just that the vehicle for our creative outlet may be ill suited, or we haven't yet discovered the right time or place to use it. We may go along for months or even years always fighting a part of ourselves, until one day we begin to understand the many trials we have undergone have had a purpose – they have tested our resolve to commit to a new life.

"A step in the wrong direction is better than staying on the same spot all your life...Once you're moving forward you can correct your course as you go."
- Maxwell Maltz

Everything that happens in life is a lesson to be learned. We don't always have to experience the lesson firsthand; however, in order to be able to benefit from it. We can learn from observing the experiences of others. In the seed of any seeming tragedy lies the fruit of good fortune.

Signs and omens don't just appear at critical times in our lives, they are always there, but often we are so preoccupied with the nitty-gritty of daily life to notice. And even when we learn to begin to pay attention it is often difficult to interpret the signs.

How do we tell if our hunches, our intuitions are genuine or if we are making them up? Usually, in my case, the answer or sign will be something that surprises me and is not something I would "normally" think. If I doubt the sign or message I move in that direction anyway. Now that's a lie. I don't always; sometimes I argue and ask for clarification. I've learned through the years my soul likes this, appreciates this. They are there to work with us, not to move us around like pawns on a chessboard. These lives we are living are meant to be co-created between our souls and us. The intuitive messages from our souls are only suggestions not orders.

When you receive an urge, a feeling, a message from the soul, say like the feeling you are to move, change jobs, leave a relationship, it is important to know you have a right to say to your soul: Conditions under which I could do that are, and write out the things you feel would make it possible for you to do what the soul is suggesting more comfortably. For years, once I was in conscious contact with my soul, I tried to do everything I felt was being suggested. I thought these messages were direct orders from God, from my soul. It took years and coming to a point of emotional, physical and financial exhaustion before the soul explained to me their messages were only suggestions and I had a right to argue, bargain or state conditions under which I would attempt to do what was being suggested.

If I've written out what I desire, I can more easily take a leap of faith when the opportunity arises, because I've written out my desires and released them with: I now accept this or something better, through the grace of God, and to the highest good of all concerned. Therefore, I can trust this leap of faith is going to take me in the direction of my goal, even though there is no obvious evidence this is so.

I'm reminded of the *Raiders of the Lost Ark* and Indiana Jones and the Last Crusade movies. The bridge never appeared until he took the first step into the void. In my case, it always seemed the net didn't appear until I was in midair.

Often when I take a leap of faith, I'm not only opening a door, I'm getting out of the way so the Universe can perform the next step. Sometimes the message is "wait," which is the hardest one for me. But somehow, by letting things be, and having events take their natural course, we unfetter the invisible forces that direct individual progress—doors open and the way is made clear.

How can we tell when we are in the "flow" and when we are just taking the path of least resistance? If you have written out what you desire your life to be about and what you desire to have happen and you are following: What is the next single thing for me to do or know for me to be in a state of divine grace? Then you can be comfortable knowing the path will have little resistance. If you are just taking the easy way out of a dilemma, without asking if this is the next single thing for me to do to be in a state of divine grace, you can be sure there will be a 2 by 4 event to live through on the path you have chosen.

Life is not a problem to be solved, but a mystery to be lived. If we get this and understand our life is to be a co-creation, we can enjoy the mystery, somewhat control the 2 by 4 events by watching for the signs of the feathers, and if we write out what we desire our lives to be about. The more we do this, the easier it becomes to recognize the positive values in what appear to be the negative moments and aspects of our lives. When traffic is stopped and our flow is interrupted, we can begin to realize we are being saved from being involved in an accident by being detained or we can rail at "traffic," which I can assure doesn't give a damn about your schedule. Accepting divine timing and patience are two of our greatest lessons.

Insight is the ability to accept events and to learn from the process of life, as it unfolds. Hindsight gives us access to seeing the pattern as it has unfolded and clues as to how to avoid the same type of lesson events in the future. Coincidences are by no means meaningless random events, but rather are clues as to how the Universe is organized and we should pay attention to the coincidences or synchronicities in our lives. There truly are no accidents, except the accidents of timing and chance that converge to produce meaningful results in our lives when they are most needed to get our attention.

How different it would be when something bad happens to us instead of asking: "Why me?" we ask. "Who is responsible?" and "It isn't fair!" And "Why did this happen?" And "What kind of God would allow this to happen?" And we voice countless other comments and questions. It is said "true enlightenment occurs when one is able to accept miracles and miseries with equal detachment, knowing, feeling and responding to them as one and the same voyages of the human spirit." Higher consciousness, however, does not mean a cessation of physical or emotional pain. Eliminating our expectations of other people can eliminate much emotional pain. Paying attention to our bodies and to our intuition can eliminate much physical pain. Our attitudes control much of what happens in our lives. If we see the world and all that is in it as corrupt, our acts will be based in fear and guilt, but if we see the world and ourselves as positive manifestations of God, based on acceptance, rightness, and a sense of belonging, our general outlook will be brighter and healthier.

We have no time for game playing, no time to put ourselves down, or to entertain thoughts of resentment, hatred, or retaliation. If we participate in these actions we cancel out everything we came to learn about love, compassion and forgiveness. Disappointment is real, but it happens more often when we have unrealistic expectations of others.

Expecting everyone to treat you fairly is like expecting a lion not to attack you because you are a vegetarian.

Earth is a school. We came here to learn lessons and to remember what we know from other lives. In spiritual growth we go forward, then backward a bit, then forward again. Like everything else we learn, it's as though we have to experience the lesson over and over until we finally own it. Each time we experience the lesson, if we don't resist, if we surrender, we get through it more quickly, more easily. And we are free to go on to the next lesson. There will always be lessons. It is our attitude and resistance that determines how difficult our life is going to be. The more we are able to live in the present moment, the more enlightenment is experienced, without a struggle, without trying, without striving.

Maharishi Mahesh Yogi, guru of Transcendental Meditation, teaches there are four stages of enlightenment that usually, but not always, develop sequentially: Cosmic Christ Consciousness, God consciousness, unity consciousness and Brahman consciousness. These are experiential states, not easy to describe but, to over simplify, perhaps Cosmic Christ Consciousness refers to that state when one becomes a purely objective observer of all the thoughts and events occurring in one's life when one is "in the world but not of the world." God consciousness occurs when one becomes acutely and permanently aware of God's presence behind everything that is. Unity consciousness is the state in which one's awareness has assimilated total knowledge and knows the sum of all knowledge is everything is, literally, One. And lastly, Brahman consciousness is that ultimate state of awareness when one's individuality has disappeared into God's (Brahma's) greater awareness so that one says, "I am God, you are God, all is God."

We are all part of an immense organic system; Creation. We all have a destiny to fulfill. We chose this destiny before we came into this incarnation. Therefore, there is a path each of us is to follow. We do, however, make that path up as we go along, depending on our attitudes, our choices and the intentions we set for ourselves. As breath gives life to the body, so there is a spiritual pulse which throbs through the human organism, sustaining the cosmic rhythm and universal harmony, linking every man and woman with their soul and with each other.

"What you do may seem insignificant, but it's very important that you do it."
- Mahatma Gandhi

The path of spiritual growth is littered with the residue of discarded relationships. That does not mean the relationships were wrong or unwise – it simply means they outlived their usefulness. Our paths will take us sometimes together and sometimes apart, but all paths lead us back to ourselves. Each of us is responsible for the image of God we allow to dominate and guide us. The World truly is a cosmic conspiracy created to delight, teach and transform us. If we stay conscious, if we stay in the moment and not in the past or the future there is the possibility for more joy.

There are only three ways to change the direction of our lives for better or worse: crisis, chance and choice. Our lives at this moment are the result of the choices we've made up to this point. We've either paid attention to the feather-like messages of our intuition and made choices in favor of our soul contracts or we've been battered by the 2 by 4 method of crisis to move ourselves in the direction of our original soul intention. Unconscious choice is the way we end up living other people's lives. By not choosing, we allow others to make decisions for us. This leaves us room to blame someone else if we are unhappy. Life is not predestined; it is a result of constant choice. People who have difficulty making decisions do not trust their instincts, their intuition.

"Regrets are as personal as fingerprints."
– Margaret Culkin Banning

A wrong choice is not necessarily a bad choice. Spirit never asks more of us than that we do the best we can in the moment. All choices are redeemable. Just because we feel we failed at a relationship doesn't mean it was a failure. We learned many lessons from it. I don't think Spirit asks us to choose between doing what's right and what's wrong so much as to choose between loving and learning. Sometimes it's very difficult to know which choice to make to move toward our destiny, especially if it involves an upheaval in your life and the lives of those you touch. When that happens, it is important to ask ourselves, "What would Love do?" If we do the loving thing we will learn without the 2 by 4. Most of the time, when we've made a bad choices, we can look back in hindsight and remember at the deepest intuitive level we knew we should not even be entertaining the thought of this choice. Usually we were running away from something else when we made these choices. It is important to occasionally ask ourselves: If I died tonight what would I regret not having done?

"The past is not only that which happened but also that which could have happened but did not."
– Tess Gallagher

Sometimes the feather message comes as what I call divine discontent. You can't put your finger on what's wrong, but you just don't feel right. You know you should be doing something different, but you just can't figure out what it is. It sometimes feels like someone tightening the screws on my mind or emotions, like my actual space is shrinking. The discontent can first begin to show up in our lives as disorder. Often in watching myself allow the disorder I see I'm resisting a message that is trying to come through from my soul. If I choose to begin to rectify the order, clarity will come. I may not like the clarity, because obviously I've been avoiding the clarity by allowing the disorder. When the clarity comes I am always left with the choice. What do I do with this knowledge of how I am sabotaging myself? I can walk away from the assignment, but not from the lesson. The lesson will continue to come in as many disguises as is necessary until I learn it. I can continue to ignore it or not act on it and wait for the 2 by 4 version of the message or the brick wall.

When we get the feeling it is time to let go of something, whether it is a job, relationship, object or desire, it's like a time warning signal that says. "You have ten days left. After that, your soul's going to do it." So the desire to hold on is not going to stop the process of change, your process of growth... you know it's true. You can heed the signal or wait for the 2 by 4. The only choice seems to be to do it willingly, on our own timetable, which at least gives us advance warning, or do it on destiny's schedule, which is never convenient. Spirit is determined we will learn one way or another. I don't think there is a more frightening feeling in the World than the moment before surrendering to one's destiny when it involves other people.

Every day we experience death. It may be the death of dreams, misconceptions, illusions, enthusiasm, vitality, hope, courage, faith or trust. More often than any of us ever expect life shocks and stuns us with the sudden death of a loved one, a devastating diagnosis, a conversation that begins with the chilling words, "There's something I've got to tell you." These conversations change the direction of our lives ready or not. Life as we knew it is over. But the truth is, if we had stayed conscious, if we had been paying attention to our intuition, our soul, we would have been aware this change was coming and could have prepared ourselves and made choices in favor of ourselves.

People are always blaming their circumstances for what they are. I don't believe in circumstances. The people who get on in this World are the people who get up and look for the circumstances they desire, and, if they can't find them, make them.
- George Bernard Shaw

We are meant to live through our circumstances and learn from them, not stay stuck in them.

"How many times does Spirit whisper, one, two, three, work with Me? Every day, every hour, probably every minute. But do we hear? Are we listening? Sometimes it's the very frustration of our stumbling that provides us with the detour we need to get back on track toward our authenticity. Stop limiting Spirit. Work with Divine Intelligence and be grateful God doesn't think like us."
- Sarah Ban Breathnach

Spirit speaks to us in many ways through others, TV, radio, billboards, dreams, feelings, flashes of insight, songs, books, magazines, even license plates. Spirit will use anything available in front of us to get the message to us if we are paying attention. Remember in your own life an "ah ha" moment, when the static cleared and suddenly you were aware of Divine Intervention in your life, suddenly you knew what to do and you knew you weren't alone. You were willing to follow the soul-directed impulse. Sarah Ban Breathnach calls it "the soul's Morse code—the dots and dashes of our daily round, so often dismissed as meaningless – not only connects, but resonates on the deepest level." Remember those times when you feel overwhelmed, confused, and afraid and chances are the fog will lift and you will know your next direction.

We betray ourselves when we stay put even though we know we should push past. When we stumble but don't get up, when we deny what and whom we love. When we let others choose for us we deny our souls. We live lives other than the ones we came to Earth to live. Watch and feel for the feather messages of your soul, avoid the 2 by 4 lessons and the brick walls. Live the loving, creative, joy-filled life you were born to live.

If you wish to pursue more information on this subject I recommend:
Sarah Ban Breathnach's *Simple Abundance* and *Something More*
Dennis F. Augustine's *Gifts from Spirit – A Skeptic's Path*

10.

The Brain And The Mind

The mystery of the beginning of life on Earth has never been solved. In the beginning, reproduction was a simple matter. Protoplasmic cells simply multiplied and separated and renewed themselves, possessing immortality. Then there came into being a new mode of begetting, sexual generation, and with this new mode of reproduction came death.

As the process of Human evolution continued, the forms of Humans became ever more complex. Through millenniums the Human brain developed under the impact of the evolving soul to its current state. It is currently an instrument radiating certain mental wavelengths, but capable of producing more spiritual wavelengths. The Human brain is now capable of abstract thought and able to interact with Universal Mind. Our minds are now able to absorb the properties of our soul and capable of union with the divine Spirit, the eternal part of ourselves.

BIRTH OF THE SEED MIND

When the form of the Human first came into existence on the Earth its state was almost as crude as that of the gorilla. The brains of the two forms were practically the same. The Human brain has evolved, and the gorilla brain has remained the same. The difference is consciousness.

The Human is an immortal soul inhabiting a physical form endowed with the potential of progression toward godhood. The gorilla remains a species of animal not blessed with an individual soul, but a member of a group animal soul.

Universal Mind operating through the evolving physical forms of

Humans has caused Humans to evolve according to the original pattern to which Humans were meant to evolve and are continuing to do so. The Human body, far from perfect now, is expected to evolve to complete perfection, according to the auric pattern invisible in the ethers surrounding it. God gifted Humans with Mind and consciousness.

Even the most primitive Human brain registers the processes of imagination, memory and the power to learn, since a Human is a being with an individualized soul and mind. The electrical waves are different between Humans and animals.

HUMAN'S DIVINE POTENTIAL

Humans are destined to evolve into godhood and the womb of spiritual growth is the physical body. The physical body comes forth with the capacity to see, hear, feel; taste and smell, but the soul must use these physical forms again and again as its womb of spiritual development. The soul returns countless times to inhabit a physical form so the Human, through the process of evolution, can continue its long journey of becoming spiritual.

Science declares the Human brain to be the greatest instrument a Human possesses, housing the entire thinking mechanism. The mystic declares the brain to be only a composite of certain cells, convolutions of neurons acting as an instrument of the mind which, in turn, acts as an agent for the invisible soul which is the property of the Spirit, sent down into the World of matter to gain experience in the school of life. The soul is becoming divine through these life experiences and upon graduation into its ultimate divinity; it will unite again with the Spirit. At that time, the soul will no longer have the need to branch out from the Oversoul since having completed its purpose.

Microscopically speaking, discovering the mind to be a thing apart from the brain does not disqualify the brain from possessing unique and miraculous possibilities. The brain presents a laboratory of infinite investigation and it is only though persistence in this investigation that a Human enriches their knowledge not only of the mind's existence but of its unlimited powers. Even though as mystics we are far more concerned with the study of the Human's mind, it behooves us to become knowledgeable to some degree concerning the brain as the instrument of the mind.

Humans do not think with their brain. We think through the brain.

We think with our mind as it operates through the glandular system and through the brain cells. The brain is a passageway of memories arising from actions of the mind and glandular system.

The brain is the enlarged portion of the cerebrospinal nervous axis contained within the skull and extending down the spinal column. The brain is the organ of consciousness, ideation and voluntary muscular control, receiving impressions from the organs of our individual senses.

The brain contains over ten billion cells. It weighs approximately three pounds and resembles a pink-gray jelly. Medical science has discovered it is **not** the size or weight of the brain which determines the intellect of the individual.

The brain does not reason, it cannot love, nor does it hate or experience sensational urges of any kind. The brain has no intellect of itself. It is the seat of the mind only insofar as the mind uses it as the principle focal point through which to function. The glandular structure and the nervous systems have no power to operate by themselves. It is the force of the mind which causes emotions to arise which can either create a better person or destroy the Human.

The power of the Human mind is limited by the brain's capacity. As the Human brain cells develop, the Human is better able to progress mentally and intellectually, but the power to progress lies not within the brain itself. The power lies in the soul and the personality that uses the glandular and nervous systems as avenues of manifestation.

The importance of the brain is accentuated when we realize we can reach awareness of the World about us only through the mechanism of our brain. Within the cerebrum are found the sensory motors of the body. Into the cerebrum, the seat of the cerebrospinal nervous system, flow impulses from the glands and the nervous system which make us aware we can see, feel, taste, hear and smell.

Diseases of the brain destroy the Human ability to use these five senses. Within the brain is the physical focal point of the Human consciousness and our ability to sense the World about us in every aspect. It is through these sense centers in the brain the Human gathers knowledge of the physical World.

The brain consists of intricate nerve tissues that communicate with each other. The brain may be divided into six parts:

1. The *cerebrum* lies in the upper regions of the skull, from front to back and forms a "skull cap" over the top part of the brain. It is called the upper brain and is the seat of active intelligence. It is a

vital part of the "the Tree of Knowledge of Good and Evil."

2. The *cerebellum* occupies the back portion of the skull and is called the little brain. It controls the activities of the voluntary muscles. The fibers in its central lobe are arranged so they form a tree-like mass of white matter called the *arbor vitae*, "Tree of Life."

3. The *medulla oblongata* lies just in front of the cerebellum and represents the beginning of the spinal cord in the neck region at the base of the skull.

4. The *brain stem* is located just above the medulla and is shaped like the knob of a walking stick.

5. The *ventricles* are the "hollow tubes" located throughout the brain and contain the brain fluids and dews.

6. The *Third Eye* includes the pituitary and pineal glands which are located at the center of the brain.

THE CEREBRUM, THE HUMAN CROWN

The cerebrum's hemisphere of the Human brain is a crown in more ways than one. Its functions set Humans apart from the animal kingdom and make Humans a co-creator with God. The circulatory, the digestive and the excretory systems are alike in Humans and animals. Humans differ from animals mostly in the region of the cerebral hemispheres which is located at the top part of the Human brain.

The cerebrum of the Human brain makes it possible for Humans to learn and to benefit from past experiences. It makes it possible to change Human behavior to what is most beneficial personally.

The cerebrum is comprised of a core of white matter completely surrounded by a layer of gray matter called the cortex. The cortex appears to be the seat of highest intelligence in the cerebral hemispheres. Within the cortex or gray matter is found the mysterious factor which gives Humans the ability to learn. It is also the sensory area of the brain.

Billions of brain cells are arranged in groupings very similar to the arrangement of stars in the heavens. The force that operates this incomparable communication system is electricity. Within the average brain exists the equivalent of about twenty watts of electric energy. The cells themselves are minute dynamos. They generate electrical charges from oxygen and body chemicals within themselves, discharging lower or higher levels of electrical energy according to the changing stimulus. Within the sum total of the cortical cells of the brain is found the physical terminal of the personality, the Human thinker.

Humans are differentiated from the animal by obvious capacity of the Human brain to receive progressive impressions of mental illumination. The animal brain is not so capable and not so constituted. The Human can become divine only by developing a brain power capable of receiving the down pouring of still higher illumination.

THE CEREBELLUM, CENTER OF COORDINATION

The cerebellum, "the little brain," is located in the rear part of the skull. It compares in size and weight to a medium-sized orange. The cerebellum is a recent evolutionary acquisition. It is not the seat of sensory perception as is the cerebrum. It can be diseased or destroyed without affecting the senses in any way, but the muscle tone of the physical form will be affected and so will muscle strength. The cerebellum is the organ which regulates equilibrium. It is the seat of coordination in the body.

There are many mysteries concerning this organ. One of these concerns its effect on the individual when, through disease or accident, some part of the cerebellum is injured. The removal of only a portion of the cerebellum results in an inability to maintain equilibrium, to walk or to maintain a sense of balance or direction. However, removal of the entire cerebellum corrects the situation and balance, direction and equilibrium are restored.

This fact understandably presented an enigma to medical science which has only recently been solved by one of its most amazing discoveries: the Human nervous system is in the midst of shifting its present position.

The cerebellum is shifting toward the front of the head and its functions are being transferred to the brain stem.

The shift of the spinal column when Humans began to walk erect made space available in the skull. The brain began developing new areas and some of this development is still proceeding which is the shift of the cerebellum toward the front of the head and a change in the brain stem located just in front of the cerebellum. It is this incredible "network" in the brain stem that assumes control and takes command when the cerebellum is removed completely.

THE BRAIN STEM, THE SEAT OF INSTINCTS

Lower vertebrates (animals having a backbone) possess the brain stem and actually, in many cases, their only development is found in the brain stem. Most animalistic instincts are housed in it. Here, the Human and animal share a common ground for the brain stem, which contains the seat of the Human's primitive instincts.

It is the portion of the brain that first developed in the Human. Instincts arise from the sensory organs which end in the ganglia, or nerve cell clusters, of the brain stem. Animals primarily live their lives according to these brain stem perceptions and instincts. Humans, on the other hand, develop their individual personality in the cerebrum, as do the higher vertebrates, such as dolphin, cat, dog, monkey, ape and horse.

The brain stem enables Humans to see, feel, hear, touch and smell, but without the developed cerebrum a Human would not be aware of these sensory abilities. With only the brain stem the Human could see but would not recognize what they saw. A Human would see their mother for instance, but not recognize her as their mother unless, the sense of sight were carried to the seat of perception, the occipital lobes located in the back of the head.

Psychology has divided Humans into two main species:
1. The brain stem personality — the Human that lives and governs their life according to their animal instincts and perceptions; as opposed to,
2. The cortical personality — the individual who lives according to their future desires.

THE MEDULLA OBLONGATA-MATRIX OF THE HUMAN'S INNER MAGIC

The medulla oblongata is the connecting link between the spinal cord and the brain. Where the spinal cord meets the brain it widens out, forming the medulla oblongata and the brain stem. The medulla actually could be referred to as the upper end of the spinal cord although it is considerably larger in proportion.

The medulla oblongata is shaped like an inverted pyramid. It comprises the central station of the nervous system. In this station lie the vital centers for respiration, blood pressure, muscle tension and numerous other functions. If a person's neck is broken and any of these vital centers are damaged, death occurs immediately.

THE MEDULLA AND THE HOLY BREATH

The medulla holds in its body the fibers from a cluster of nerve cells which comprise the vagus nerve trunk, a nerve center. The medulla nerve center is one of the most supremely important in the entire body, both biologically and physiologically. The nerve plexuses in the medulla extend downward into the spinal cord and connect with the breathing mechanism.

The ancients considered this the channel for the holy breath in Humans. The vagus reaches a terminal point in the heart of the medulla. It extends downward to terminate again in the right auricle of the heart so that the heart ethers are transmitted to the medulla by this supreme nerve.

THE MYSTIC FIRE OF THE MEDULLA SOUL NOTE

Every object of the universe emits a cosmic sound. The same is true of every personality, according to the radiation of the Human's particular aura which is a record or "book of judgment" pertaining to the past and progression of the individual.

There is a *soul note* in the medulla oblongata of every individual that is the note on the cosmic keyboard which harmonizes with that Human's own spiritual and personalized "music of the spheres."

Depending on this mysterious soul note and its vibrational quality, their new body is constructed as the incarnating entity enters the atmosphere of the Earth plane at the time of physical rebirth. The note sounds forth not too long following conception. The vibrational quality of the soul note attracts into the matrix of the forming etheric body, in the womb of the mother, the type of atoms that will be harmonious, those necessary to build the best possible physical vehicle for the incoming soul, according to the karma ready to be resolved, and according to the missions to be accomplished during the approaching incarnation.

The medulla sound originates in the Oversoul; the note in the medulla is only a faint echo of that higher "music." It sounds like a faint humming sound one might hear near telephone wires.

The medulla is a supreme spiritual altar in the Human form. The power and potency of the medulla flame can be influenced by the inner life of the individual. According to the way a Human "thinks in their heart," acts in their daily life and reacts to their emotional impacts, the medulla flame either burns more radiantly or fades to an ember and loses its "light of life," in which case the sound of the soul note becomes almost imperceptible.

There are several methods of fueling the medulla fire and of raising the vibrational sound of the soul note:

1. The conscious intake of solar prana and directing it to the brain.
2. Stimulating the mind by continuing to study lessons or books that create thought forms of a higher mental quality. Such study builds both mind and brain power and develops powers of concentration.
3. Consuming as many uncooked foods as seems practical for an individual's need so that the vital fires of life found in raw food is transferred to their physical body. To fill the body exclusively with dead foods is to deprive the body of the natural fire of the vegetable kingdom.
4. Serving God, Humans and the Spiritual Hierarchy to the best of one's ability, time, means and talents.

The word "medulla" signified "marrow" to the ancients and in their Mysteries the marrow of the bone was extremely significant. The medulla plays an important part in the inner Mysteries.

THE BRAIN VENTRICLES

Medical science calls the brain a tubular structure, which is to say there are hollows, or tubes in its interior. These hollows or tubes are called ventricles, and they are filled with mysterious fluids and gases about which medical science knows very little.

Medical science recognizes five ventricles. The first and second lie to the right and left of the cerebral cortex. The third ventricle is placed in the center of the brain; the fourth lies to the rear of the head and below the third ventricle while the fifth becomes the lateral ventricle near the thalamus.

Mystics recognize the ultimate possibility of seven ventricles, the last two being composed of the four ethers of the physical plane. They extend down the tiny, microscopic tube of the spinal cord which we call sushumna.

The brain fluids are formed in the ventricles and circulate slowly downward through the brain stem tube, some portion seeping finally into the spinal cord itself.

In the convolutions of the brain are found other centers which will one day become vortices of power as Humans continue to unfold spiritually, until eventually the head area itself will represent a small universe, the sun being the pineal gland and the moon the pituitary.

HUMANS HAVE THREE BRAINS

Humans have three brains:
1. the *superior brain* in the head region
2. the *solar plexus* in the abdomen
3. the *root brain* in the gonads

It is important that we understand the functions of the solar plexus and root brain which register their influence upon the evolution of the Human's mental force field. These are secondary centers, subject to control by centers in the superior brain, once the solar plexus and root brain centers are developed.

THE HUMAN SOLAR PLEXUS BRAIN

The *solar plexus center* is the dominating plexus of the sympathetic nervous system as well as the seat of the astral-emotional body. This emotional center can well be called a brain, for the thoughts of the majority dwell principally in their emotional plexus. Energy follows thought, and the solar plexus is a center of tremendous thought-force.

This great nerve center in the pit of the stomach is the storehouse of electrical prana. It is well named the solar plexus, for from it radiate pranic rays which flow to all parts of the body, much as the sun radiates energy to all its planets. It is a control station for operating the subconscious mind, under the dominion of the pituitary.

From this brain rise the baser emotions, ugly specters of the lower self. It is the seat of all negative sensations like hate, anger, envy, anxiety, jealousy, grief, worry and fear. Knowing this we can use rhythmic breathing, directing prana to the solar plexus brain to quiet the nerves, soothe the mind and promote inner tranquility. Prana is the "medicine" of the ethers.

It is from this sensitive solar region we feel our heartbreak, rather than from the heart itself. Its influence extends even into the region of the throat, causing the "lump in the throat" experienced when we have been under emotional duress, this lump being constricted, tense muscles.

This solar brain contains our voice of conscience. This conscience is the most important inner directive of our lives, so far as our instincts are concerned, if we would but heed it. Its guidance, however, does not stem from intuition, reason or logic; it wells up from within instinct, the voice of past training.

When the personality has erred in some previous incarnation and has suffered long in paying off some karmic debt, a memory of it is reflected from the superconscious into this solar network. It upraises to haunt us as the voice of conscience if we are tempted to make the same error in this life.

THE ROOT BRAIN

The *root brain* involves the gonads which are the generative organs, the testes of the male and the ovaries of the female.

The *root brain* is not to be confused with the root chakra which is located in the prostate region in the male and the uterus in the female.

Under pituitary stimulation, the gonadic root brain produces the reproductive fluids, seed substance and hormones, which combine to become the creative energies that rise up the spinal cord in rhythmic cycles. When the influence of this etheric force strikes the solar plexus brain, it produces the urge to create. These creative energies can be utilized toward building a more powerful brain or they can be dissipated in copulation, according to the interpretation the individual places upon the urge.

We are not to seek to destroy the urge but to attempt to transmute a portion of its etheric force out of the generative organs into the part of the brain that is used for mental and creative activities.

THE ROOT CHAKRA

The root chakra is not the same as the root brain. The root brain covers the gonadic reproductive area; the root chakra interpenetrates the prostatic area in the male and the uterus in the female. This chakra houses the kundalini.

The *root chakra*, with the mysterious kundalini, consists of primary forces which radiate in four directions: one up, one down and two horizontal, causing the chakra to appear as if a cross penetrated its center. A great portion of the kundalini force enters the root chakra from the spleen, drawn inward from the ethers around us, through the soles of the feet, drawn upward from the Earth. Much of the kundalini force in the root chakra flows downward to enter and stimulate the gonads.

The *kundalini*, composed of the electronic forces and energies of the root chakra, represents the duel "serpent" of the mystics. Mystics recognize that there is a serpent of carnality and a serpent of wisdom. Kundalini represents both. It is the fire which helps stir the gonads to their procreative activity. It is the fire, pouring into the gonadic root brain, that causes the production of the seed substance (sperm) and semen (fluid) in the gonads, and which activates the pressure which nature usually releases through copulation. In the female, kundalini fertilizes the ovum or egg released by the ovary.

The undirected and unchecked fire of kundalini, flowing down to stimulate the gonads, becomes the serpent of carnality. When directed upward and aroused to the full power, kundalini, rising up sushumna like a brilliant river of light to the head centers, becomes the serpent of wisdom, to be utilized as brain power by the creative genius.

GOD IN MATTER VERSUS GOD IN MIND

The root brain in the gonads represents God-in-matter. The superior brain in the head represents God-in-mind.

Until a Human transforms the creative energies in the reproductive centers to the creative energies of the head centers, the generative organs will continue to consume a major portion of the creative powers. The root brain, the Human's God-in-matter, will dominate the Human's Earthly activities until the God-in-mind becomes supreme in their life.

In the present stage of Human evolution, the head centers are not fully awakened. Everything in the Human's daily life conspires to restrict the upward flow of kundalini. It is obstructed by the etheric webs which interweave each chakra. It is further blocked by the will of the Humans who presently have no desire to conserve the creative force unaware that they even should.

It is only as the creative energies of kundalini are shifted upward into the superior brain that the physical form is regenerated, and the mind attains the level of the superconscious.

THE MIND

Even though a new brain is born with each new incarnation, this is not true of the mind. The mind existed prior to conception and is birthed into the present incarnation.

Understanding the complexities of the mind is as difficult as understanding electricity. One can perform the simple act of turning on an electric light and it is accepted by us as a common event. It is only when we think of power, the forces and the activity behind the electric light that we begin to be aware of the mystery involved.

Scientists explain to us the force is electricity, but they do not tell us what electricity is. It is the same with the mind and the brain. Scientists tell us the brain is the seat of the cerebrospinal nervous system which in turn, is the house of the mind. But they do not tell us what the mind is. They simply tell us what the brain is.

Knowledge of the brain is far from knowledge of the mind, the mysterious storehouse which uses the brain as the power of electricity uses the light bulb for its illumination.

The brain, like the light bulb, is dead without the power behind it to make it function. The light bulb lights at the flick of a switch. The brain lights up at the flick of the mind.

THE MENTAL FORCE FIELD

The Mind, to function in the material World, first must build an instrument. That instrument is the Human brain. The Mind can build in the World of affect only from what level the soul has evolved. The soul, in turn, is higher than the Mind. In each personality it has inhabited, it has evolved different degrees of brain power so that the Mind, the agent of the soul, must build the brain according to the exact blueprint dictated by the mental evolutionary status of the soul. The individual personality, through many lives, has built a certain mental force field surrounding the brain conditioned by the Human's experiences and mental evolution.

The brain, built into the physical form at each new incarnation, is simply the house constructed by the Mind according to the evolved blueprint. The Mind can build no greater brain than what the soul, through past experience, has evolved or created.

The mental force field existed before the brain existed and was the pattern upon which the brain was constructed. Its forces built and are still building the brain through which the Mind force expresses. The mind permeates every cell of the brain but is able to operate apart from it.

The Human is a spirit possessing a soul, a mind and a body, using all these composite parts to create a whole being, a being containing both matter and spirit.

The *spirit* sends down, or projects into the realms of ether, a representative of itself which we call the soul. The *soul*, projects into the World of matter, a representative of itself, which we call the *physical body and the personality*. It builds through experience, a force field of mental substance surrounding the brain. We call that force field the Mind which is an agent of the soul.

The soul is that part of the Human which is developing and unfolding. The spirit, on the other hand, is the divine Monad (the combination of soul, spirit, and superconscious). The soul evolves according to the experiences of the personality, in the body, and takes to itself an increased degree of consciousness with each incarnation. The soul, unfolding through the agency of the mind, or mental force field, eternally evolves from incarnation to incarnation.

The brain without the Mind is a dead thing, a mass of substance without life or light.

11.

Spiritual Pilgrimages and Their Gifts

People often feel the urge to travel, to go to another country, a little-known part of the World or even just to a remote place or location. Frequently they have no logical reason for wanting to go.

Indeed, if the desire is not to return to their place of origin or childhood to attend a reunion, a funeral, a family gathering, a conference or school, or some similar function, people can find such urgings hard to accept.

In fact, if such persons do not truly understand their multi-dimensionality, it is easy to disregard such promptings because no "logical explanation" accompanies them. It is simple to brush away the desires with such justifications as, "I don't have the money to go, no time, too far away, don't want to go alone," and a hundred others. People actually believe these excuses are the real reasons for "squelching" the urgings.

Spiritual growth happens in a spiral. When it is time for us to move up to the next rung of the spiral, it is often encouraged by our soul that we return to the place of our birth or to reconnect with the vehicle through which we came to Earth, the body of our mother. This makes sense to me if I look at the energy as operating in a spiral. If I complete one cycle, by returning to the beginning, I slip easily into the next octave of energy operation. That doesn't mean I like to return to my place of birth and my physical Mother is not still in this dimension. Sometimes while we are shifting from one energy octave to the next it feels like we have lost communication with our souls, our guides, and our higher self. This can feel like the dark night of the soul. If we understand what is happening, we can understand that the wires are down, because we are being rewired to reach a higher vibration and we can endure or wait out the change more gracefully.

Occasionally our souls will ask us in meditation or through a channel to travel to certain places. We may or may not understand why we are to travel to these locations. Sometimes we only know we feel drawn to certain areas. Sometimes we just choose, seemingly from a non-spiritual perspective to take a vacation somewhere. But, usually, these trips are actually spiritual pilgrimages. Our soul wishes to pick up or deposit energy in a certain location. Sometimes other members of our Oversouls will have incarnated on Earth and reached a level of enlightenment that allows them to realize when other members of the same Oversoul come to Earth, at a later time; they will need larger amounts of energy or consciousness to accomplish their mission. Those who realize this, agree to leave a portion of their consciousness hermetically sealed in this dimension at the location they happen to be in when they leave their body through death. When we later travel to that location, for whatever reason, the symbols in our energy field unlock the hermetic seal and we gain the energy and consciousness that has been left behind.

At the time the merger happens, we may or may not be aware anything happened. Sometimes we just feel strange, or have chill bumps, or a hot flash or tears. My reaction at times has been so strong as to send me to my knees for several minutes in tears. Whatever happens and whatever reaction takes place is not as important as the fact the merger has taken place.

Each time I've been sent on a spiritual pilgrimage of this sort, I've gained a tremendous spiritual gift as a result of the merger. The first time I did it consciously, I was asked to go to the middle of the Amazon jungle of Peru. I was in Lubbock, Texas visiting my children who then lived with their father, when the message came from my soul I was to go to Amarillo, Texas and to have a reading with a woman named "Bubbles." Many times in my travels I had been given the names of people I was to find and offer them readings, but the soul always gave me more information than just a nickname. It occurred to me to call a friend who lives in Amarillo and ask her if she knew anyone named "Bubbles."

When I called and asked the question my friend laughed and said she knew Bubbles and the woman was a psychic. I got the phone number and called immediately for an appointment. The next day when I was to leave Lubbock a blizzard had occurred during the night and the roads were supposedly closed, but I proceeded to drive to Amarillo even though the center line was not visible and there where many cars and trucks in the ditches along the road. It felt as if I had Angels keeping me on the correct side of the road.

When I arrived at Bubble's door she was astonished I had come through the storm and she said because I had made the effort she would do a really good job for me. Of course, being who I am as a cynic, I wondered what she usually did for others if I was to get special treatment. She led me to a small bedroom, which was filled with left over cigarette smoke. She had an osculating fan running, but it only rearranged the smoke. Bubbles looked like what I had in my mind about psychics when my soul had first suggested I become one. Her body barely fit into the lawn chair she sat in. There was a coffee stained wooden folding table between us. She continued to smoke.

She first asked me to fill out some small pieces of paper with the names and birthdates of people in my family. From the information on the papers she did a mini astrological reading. I don't really understand astrology and especially the verbiage kind of bypasses my mind. So I just sat quietly and thought I was probably there to read for her. After the astrological part she handed me a deck of Tarot cards to shuffle, which I did. She separated them into three stacks and then rejoined them into one. She laid out the cards into some kind of order I didn't recognize since I had never had a Tarot reading. She began to talk about the cards. She told me about the card that represented me and then she said I see there are five men in your life. I corrected her and said that wasn't true now I had narrowed my relationships to just one man.

"Well, let's see maybe you were not concentrating when you shuffled the cards," she offered.

"These cards represent your relationships. This one represents Edward, this one David, this one Robert, this one John, and this one represents your son."

I was astonished and impressed she could tell the name of the person each card represented, something I was sure I could not do. I said they must be the right cards because those are the names of people with whom I have had relationships. She finished with the cards and said she would now look in the crystal dove on the corner of the table. She did not use a crystal ball.

"I see a flock of white birds," she offered.

"What does that mean?" I asked.

"It usually means a person has had a past life in Atlantis," she said, but hesitated. "Now there is another image of a dark-skinned woman sitting in a grass hut in the middle of the jungle. She says she wants you to come there she needs to give you some things before she leaves her body. She says you are from the same Oversoul."

I thought to myself, "Lady you are really good at Tarot, but you're not so great at getting images from a crystal. No one in the jungle needs to see me. And even if they did they could channel the information to me and if there are artifacts involved they could get them to me by UPS."

"I don't understand. Where is she, what jungle?" I said.

Where I was seated there was a World map on the wall behind me. She asked me to stand and to tell her the name of the orange country at the top of South America. I told her it was Peru and she said that's where she is. Then she asked me to tell her the name of the city there. I said it's Puerto Maldonado.

"The woman says she is 15 miles southeast of Puerto Maldonado and that you need to come soon because it's time for her to leave her body."

I did not consider the validity of what she said. I read for her, paid her and left to drive on to Denver. During the next few nights my meditations were interrupted by a vision of a dark-skinned woman sitting in a grass hut in the middle of the jungle. I am not your jungle kind of girl so the whole idea was appalling to me. Since the vision did not go away I took time to write out what it would take for me to be willing to do what my soul was indicating,

I demanded a paid for round trip ticket, someone fun to travel with me, perfect clothes to wear, perfect ground transportation, perfect places to stay in Peru, perfect food to eat there and I pointed out that I would not go into the jungle with straight hair. My soul would have to create a curling iron that did not require electricity. I thought this last demand would keep me from having to go to the jungle. Instead within a few days the soul made me aware of a curling iron that was fueled by butane cartridges. A week later I reconnected with a friend who said the trip was already planned and that she was to pay for me to go. As a result of that trip I received prior to Earth memory to know where I was and the circumstances of my agreement to come to Earth.

The trip to Egypt was life changing. I felt I came back a different person, a person I didn't recognize. I didn't, at the 3-D level, understand how to be this person. It took months to adjust to that change. All I can say is that I somehow became more of who I truly am. It wreaked havoc with my 3-D life in that relationships fell away and I had to create a whole new social structure within which to operate. I had received a reading many years ago by a man in Oregon, whose name I do not remember, who had told me that I was connected to a group of beings who brought the original symbols, now thought of as the Egyptian hieroglyphics, to Earth. We taught the members, of what we now think of as the Egyptian civilizations, how to use the symbols in formulas, combined with tones and energy frequencies to build the pyramids and other monolithic structures. He said we later planted the Rosetta stone so archeologists would assume that they had discovered a way to identify the hieroglyphics as an alphabet. This kept them from actually remembering the formulas and how the symbols can be used to accomplish what we would think of as miraculous events. I never deliberately have readings through other people. This reading was paid for and insisted on by a friend. During the reading our phone connection was bad because of a storm. I tried to be polite, but I must admit I thought the guy was nuts. I could not in any way relate to the reading.

My next long distance trip was to Japan and as a result of that trip I gained access to the Universal Language of Light and started doing soul symbol paintings for people. His reading began to make more sense.

When we moved into this location of the Namaste Center here in Oklahoma City, in cleaning up the backyard I turned over a flat slab of rock. The backside of the rock is covered with engraved Egyptian hieroglyphics. The sign was clear; we are in the right place. I don't presume to understand what this means entirely at the 3-D level.

A more recent trip involved going to France, Germany and Switzerland to anchor more of the feminine consciousness of God on the planet. In Germany, I merged with a soul aspect in a cemetery. The man's name on his tombstone was Bach. Many years ago I was told by my soul "Bach" will help you with the writing. Because the first metaphysical book I ever read was Richard Bach's book *Illusions*, I assumed this was the Bach spirit had referred to, but since that never happened and I later met his uncle Marcus Bach I assumed it was Marcus who would help me. He refused and later died. So I gave up the idea they would help me and just went on my way. Now this merger took place in Germany and it may or may not have anything to do with my ability to write. I have now written twelve books about metaphysics and my spiritual journey.

What has come, since the Europe trip, is an experience of the opening of a new room in my spiritual consciousness. The door is open about ten inches. When I look into the room, downloading of information, in golden light Universal Light Language symbols is taking place. If you saw the movie *Matrix* you have some idea of what this looks like. If you didn't see the movie you may have seen other visual effects of digital information being downloaded into a computer. It is downloading at a rate that is impossible for the Human mind to read and it is in symbols. As yet, I don't know what the information is; however, on the morning of the second day

I was lead to pick up two books from the bookshelf in my bedroom where I keep the unread books sent to me by publishers. The two books were called *Voyagers Vol. 1 and 2* and are by Anna Hayes. In beginning to read the first volume I was relieved to find Anna describing the experience of having information downloaded into her consciousness in a similar way to what I was experiencing. She refers to it as Universal Keylontic Symbol Code Language. She describes it not as channeling, but as the remote transfer of electronically encoded data.

She says, "Once the encoded data has been programmed into my bio-energetic field, it would process through my neurological structure in the form of electrical impulses. Through the natural bio-chemical and electrical translation processes inherent to the Human biological form, the electronically encoded information would translate into my native language and appear in my mind as direct cognition, formatted into either word text or image pictures. I did not hear the word in my mind, as no audible sound was involved; a stream of worded information would simply flow through my mind and I could feel the words as electrical impulse patterns. Image translation came in the same way, no mental pictures, but rather I clearly felt electrical impulses that carried complete images. My mind just knew the audio or visual content of the electrical impulses, as if the impulses bypassed sensory translation and appeared as direct cognition. The information always has to do with the spiritual teachings of the Law of One."

After each trip you take, and I've taken many where I never found out the gift, you may or may not become aware of the gift or the change that will happen in your consciousness. But positive change will happen.

After the Peru trip, I was living in Mt. Shasta, CA when I began to have memories of where I was before I came to Earth. Spirit has suggested that I share with you that chapter of the book I've written called *Pentimento – Diary of a Walk-in*.

In 1986 I was still doing a lot of past life regression work with people and I was working in Denver. In meditation I regressed a young man named Rocky who showed up on another planet. It freaked me out as I was as yet unaware of who I am or where I came from. I was used to people showing me lives on Earth. The next day my soul asked me to drive to Sedona so I told the young man we would have to discontinue his lessons in learning to become a channel. He wanted to travel with me, but I explained I never took anyone with me because I never knew if I was coming back to the same city. He asked to follow me in his own car. I made it clear to him, if he did, he would have to be responsible for his own food and where he would sleep. I could not ask other people to take me in and take care of me and another person. He agreed and we drove to Sedona. The first night I stayed with a friend I had previously met in Sedona and Rocky went on to Phoenix to visit with his grandparents.

The next morning I was having breakfast at the Coffee Pot Café, a place where locals and lots of New Age people hang out, when a nice looking gentleman walked up to my table and asked to sit down and have a cup of coffee with me. I agreed and he began to ask me questions about who I am and why I was in Sedona. I thought I knew who I was and told him my name and that I was a spiritual channel, which is not unusual in Sedona. I told him I didn't know as yet why my soul had brought me to Sedona at this time. He said he had a video he would like to show me. I assured him I had seen lots of videos and inquired as to the name of his. He said, "UFO Contact the Pleiades."

I was startled because a month before I had been working in Santa Fe, NM with a woman from California. After the seminar we were presenting she asked me to do a channeling session for her patron, a very wealthy woman who lived in Santa Fe and provided my friend with an amazing home to use as a center outside of Santa Cruz, CA. I agreed to do the session even though I am not a medium for recently dead people. Her patron's son had recently committed suicide. I did the session, but of course they were so emotional afterward that they didn't think to pay me. As I walked out the door to leave the husband gave me a large, heavy book, still in its plastic wrapper. The book was entitled *UFO Contact the Pleiades*. I didn't want to know anything about UFO's or extra terrestrials and was pissed they did not pay me as I needed money for food and gas to get back to Denver. I threw the book into the back of my van unopened. So when the man told me the name of his video I didn't mention the book, but told him my friend Rocky would probably be interested in seeing the video. He told me there was a group of people meeting that night at the Coffee Pot parking lot to drive out to a woman's home who had a video player and if we wanted to join them to show up at 7:00.

When Rocky got to Sedona and we met up he was very excited about the possibility of seeing the video. We met the other people at the Coffee Pot Café and caravanned out highway 89A and as we approached Red Rock Loop Road seven space ships with green flashing lights materialized over the rim of the canyon. These were not stars in the distance or balls of light; they were saucer shaped ships. All of our cars pulled off on the shoulder of the road and we got out observing the phenomenon. All my hair was standing on end, including my pubic hair (trust me a very strange feeling). I was wishing I was alone so I could pretend this wasn't happening to me. Everyone was very excited. As fast as they had appeared they seemed to disappear. I now know they just change the vibration to be non visible to the Human eye.

We returned to our vehicles and continued on to the see the video. The video is of actual film footage of Pleiadian Beam Ships photographed by a man in Switzerland called Billy Meyer. I later read his story in the book the man in Santa Fe had given me. I was uncomfortable watching the video and trying to find out why this was happening. Rocky went outside to see if the ships were still there and came back in whispering to me, "You need to talk to them." I said, "Rocky, leave me alone and let me finish watching this film so I can figure out why this is happening and besides their using your name not mine." They had begun to telepath to me, "We want to speak to Rocky. We want to speak to Rocky." I telepathed back, "So speak to Rocky and leave me the hell alone this can't have anything to do with me."

After the film was over we returned to our cars and started back into Sedona and at the same place on the highway the Mother Ship appeared over the city of Sedona. It was silent and large enough to have housed all the other ships and everyone in Sedona and Oak Creek. Again we got out of our vehicles to observe it and again all the hair stood up on my body. It seemed to disappear, just as the other ships had and we got in our vehicles and started driving toward the house where Rocky and I were to stay. Suddenly Rocky started hyperventilating because they were tapping in to his heart chakra to attempt to communicate with him. I demanded they stop and agreed to meditate after we reached the house to hear what they wanted to say to us. I was afraid Rocky was going to die in the front seat of my car tapped into by an extra terrestrial and that I would have to go to Amarillo, Texas to explain to his little Baptist mother I was very sorry her son died in my car from being tapped into by an extra terrestrial.

We finally reached the house, lit a fire in the fireplace (fortunately the home's owner was away) and we lay down in front of the fireplace to meditate. Just about the time I had gotten comfortable and breathed my way into an alpha state of consciousness there was a loud "BAM, BAM, BAM," on the front door. I must have levitated off the floor I was so startled, but Rocky jumped up to let whoever it was inside. I was concerned the ET's had come to take us away and I still didn't know who they were or what they wanted, but it was the people we had watched the movie with. They knew I am a conscious channel and they wanted us to go out to Boynton Canyon with them and to see if I could communicate with the ships. I finally surrendered and went with them.

In the meantime a dense fog had been brought in to cover the ship activity from those who should not see them. When we arrived at Boynton Canyon and got out of our cars I tuned in and brought through the message there were 27 different civilizations represented that night with ships going around and around the Earth to strengthen the magnetic grid system of the Earth. They also explained Rocky and I are extra terrestrials who have agreed to come to Earth as Human beings to assist in the evolution of Earth and Humanity and to be liaisons for the Intergalactic Federation and the Spiritual Hierarchy and the Angelic Realm. Rocky discontinued communicating with me after our trip to Sedona so I don't know what he did with his life after that experience.

From my soul I later learned that I walked in to the body I now have from a Venusian space craft in December of 1969. When we agree to come to the Earth, at this time for an assignment, we spend an apprenticeship on one of the planets or star systems in this galaxy. My apprenticeship was spent on Venus. Technically my galactic adopted parents are Lady Master Venus and Sanat Kumara. Since waking up to the fact I am an extra terrestrial impersonating a Human being to the best of my abilities and finding out I am a walk-in I've become a liaison between the Intergalactic Federation and Humans as well as a channel for the Spiritual Hierarchy of our Universe. Nothing could have been further from my reality before I woke up to my soul communication in September of 1982.

12.

The Thirteenth Step: A Guide To Spiritual Maturity And Happiness

It is never too late to ask, "Who am I? What do I really want to do with my life?" Ideally, we would ask ourselves these questions in our early twenties, in the year between high school graduation and beginning college or joining the work force. However, for whatever reason, many of us didn't ask these questions or we took someone else's answers rather than to take time to find our own. We became what our parents or society expected of us. Many people rebel at this age and refuse to "grow up" or decide to not make such difficult decisions at all. They postpone the inevitable. Most of us operate with a definition of ourselves given to us by others. We play roles without thinking, "Who is playing this role? Who am I when I am not playing a role for someone else?"

I learned this lesson only after a series of devastating events that removed all my roles. I was left bereft, sitting in a rocking chair looking out at nature with a pad and pen on my lap writing over and over, I am..? I am..? I am..? I did not realize at the time I was giving myself the answer; beyond the roles, I am the I AM, the God consciousness part of me who chooses to play certain roles in the World. **The True Definition of me and you is:**

I AM God operating through my personality for the benefit of Earth, all species of life on the Earth and beyond.

97

A spark of the energy of God causes each of our hearts to beat. Each of us came to Earth with a purpose, a life work, a calling. These purposes vary. However, some of these purposes are fundamental in nature. We came to experience life in Human bodies, to experience "otherness" of being either male or female, to experience being physical with senses. We came to enjoy the beauties of this planet. We came to bring Spirit into matter. What does that mean? We came to embody Spirit in a denser form of the Third dimension. We also agreed to create heaven on Earth. What does that mean? We agreed to be the architects of what heaven on Earth would look like and feel like in our own individualized expression of life.

Each of us came to Earth with individual gifts, talents and potential. Our childhood and time spent receiving our education gives us an opportunity to become aware of these gifts, talents and potential. If, for whatever reason, we came into families where this development was stunted or underachieved, we have a responsibility as adults to remedy this situation through exploration of ourselves, our gifts and talents at whatever age we find ourselves now. We chose the families and circumstances we came into from the level of our souls. We chose deliberately to have these teachers and opportunities or restrictions in order to prepare ourselves for our life's work.

We are like a piece of bamboo or copper tubing that eventually will be used as a flute. Each blow life presents, each nurturing, affects the quality of the reed or pipe. The dents, the scratches or the polishing we receive tempers us perfectly to be the vessels through which our voice, our creative abilities, our gifts, the voice of God, will be offered to the World. Each of us comes to Earth with a quota of people our lives are to touch. These people can only be touched by us, through the flute that has been tempered by the experiences of our particular lives. Those gifts you have to offer the World cannot be given by anyone else. The art you would create, the children, the songs, the inventions, the books, the poems, the life example, cannot be duplicated by any other person. You are unique and the World needs your gifts. Your life experience has prepared you perfectly to give yourself and your gifts to the World and, therefore, to God. It is all God. Each person we meet is a part of God expressing itself, whether that personality remembers it is God or not; it is true.

If we were born into wealth and had all the advantages of childhood, but did not experience nurturing physically or emotionally, we have a story tempered by those events. We can choose to be nurturing and emotionally available. If we were born into poverty, or an abusive lifestyle of alcoholism and sexual or physical abuse, we have a choice to see these events as courses we took to prepare us to be spiritual masters or we can see ourselves as victims. We can accept our "life" education or we can make excuses. There are no victims at the level of the soul. We are all making choices before we come into Human form and after we arrive. There is a purpose to all events. We can learn from these and use the information and experiences, or we can plead amnesia and victimhood and not fulfill our roles by overcoming and transmuting these events. We can be a part of a new form of Human that does not see addiction, abuse, acts of horror and dishonor as normal Human behavior. We can be what we see missing in the World.

To be truly happy, we must embrace both continuity and change.

Another way of expressing, bringing Spirit into matter, is to manifest, co-create or precipitate the life we desire. If you ask yourself the question, "What do I need to be happy?" You will get one answer. If you ask yourself the question, "What do I desire?" You will likely get yet another answer, if you are being truly honest with yourself, which is imperative if you are to ever be truly happy. Total self-honesty is imperative if we are to have a form of happiness that is not dictated or dependent upon the presence and behaviors of other people. If you ask yourself, "What is my heart's desire?" you will hear the truth, the truth of your soul.

Manifestation takes place through desire, belief and expectancy. Before we can use Universal Law wisely and manifest what we truly desire, our heart's desires, it is important to understand we have been using Universal Law unconsciously to create the life we are currently living. The lives we are currently living are a direct result of what we have been thinking and believing up to this point in our life. Each thing, whether it be a physical object, a relationship with a person, a bank account, a debt, a job, a home, or a health challenge, it is in our life because of a belief which precipitated a thought, which drew this situation or condition into our lives.

When you write out your desires it useful to write: "I desire, intend, deserve and now gratefully accept." Then you can describe in as much detail as possible your desire.

If you want to change your life, change the way you think.

The first step, to spiritual maturity and happiness, is to watch what we are thinking, to practice self-scrutiny, self-appraisal, self-appreciation. Within each of us there is an active observer. Whether we call this our conscience, our higher self, our inner adult, our soul or God, this part of us exists. If we begin to watch what we are thinking and verbally expressing, and realize that our subconscious mind takes our thoughts and our verbal expressions literally, we will see how we created the life we have now.

List five dissatisfactions you now have in your life:

_____
_____
_____
_____
_____

Acknowledge the negative but focus on the positive.

List five things you feel would correct these situations:

_____
_____
_____
_____
_____

We can alter our lives by the opinions we hold of our lives and ourselves.
We can only love and give to others from our own reservoir.

The second step to spiritual maturity and happiness is to take responsibility for all our thoughts.
When we begin to listen to ourselves we realize we are negative more often than we would have imagined. We are self-critical, we are critical of others, we do not treat ourselves lovingly in our thoughts and yet we expect others to love us. Jesus asked us to love our neighbors as ourselves. What he implied was we could only love our neighbors to the extent that we were able to love ourselves. Most of us have attempted to love our families and our neighbors without first loving ourselves.

We can only love and give to others from our own reservoir.

We must realize thoughts are things. What we think is what we get. If we look around the room, every object in that room was a thought before it was a thing. If we look at the World, every situation, every object, was thought by someone before it could happen or exist. If we collectively change our thinking, we can change the condition of the World. If we individually change what we are thinking, we can change our lives.

You learn who you think you are by watching what you think.
You learn to "know" yourself by listening to your soul.

The third step to spiritual maturity and happiness is to realize that manifestation is fueled by feeling.
If we feel good about ourselves we attract good things into our lives. If we enjoy being with our self, others will enjoy being with us. If we feel we deserve, others will feel we deserve. If we feel love and respect for ourselves, others will treat us with love and respect. If we feel peaceful, the World we live in will become peaceful. We must first become what we desire to experience in the World. We can seek to be that which we feel is missing in the World. If we wish to have a relationship with a well-rounded, emotionally and financially stable person, we need first to become those ourselves.

We must first feel we deserve before we can be a receiver.

The fourth step to spiritual maturity and happiness is self-honesty.
What do you really desire to do? Don't make excuses about not having enough money or education or time to do what you desire. Don't use the excuse you are too young or too old, or have too many responsibilities. Just tell me, and yourself, the truth about what you enjoy. What would you be doing if you could do anything? This will take a bit of fantasizing on your part. You can't be honest with other people until you become honest with yourself.

Begin exactly where you are now. You may be bored, employed in an unfulfilling job, unemployed, retired, in an unfulfilling relationship, in no romantic relationship, in debt, or have more money than you need but don't know how to use it to make you happy. No matter what your life is now, it is a direct result of what you have thought up to this point in your life.

List five things you enjoy doing, ways you would enjoy spending your time and serving the World and Humanity. (These do not need to be ways you "think" you could make a living, just things you enjoy doing.)

_____

_____

_____

_____

_____

The fifth step to spiritual maturity and happiness is to realize you originate your feelings and you can, therefore, change them.
When I began my spiritual journey I actually thought other people brought me my feelings and, thus, I could not control them. Our feelings are a "response mechanism" fueled by our thoughts, past experiences and beliefs.

Make a list of how you would like to feel. Suggestions: Peaceful, productive, successful (requires your definition of what success would look and feel like), financially serene (there is a difference between financial security and financial serenity), attractive, sure there is a God, sure the Universe is benevolent, playful, loved, romantic, useful, happy, calm, comfortable, expectant, hopeful, etc.

_____

_____

_____

_____

_____

The sixth step to spiritual maturity and happiness is the understanding that the only constant in the World is change.
Everything changes. That is the natural order of the Universe. Change is supposed to happen. We can only control our lives to a certain extent. Our lives are not predestined, but they are ordained. We can't control the future, but we can influence the future of our lives and the Earth through what we think, believe and focus upon. Learning to live in rhythm with the seasons of change and to welcome and plan for change relieves stress, adds enjoyment to our lives and abolishes boredom. If we live expecting change, rather than dreading it, we live in harmony with nature and the natural flow of divine order. If we resist change we will always be in a state of fear, dread, stress or pain. Our souls and nature will only allow a certain degree of control on our part to hold things rigid or stagnant. Change will happen. Growth requires change. Change requires courage.

Change is the only constant.

The seventh step to spiritual maturity and happiness is to realize we are placed on Earth to be co-creators with God, to be the architects of our own lives and to assist in creating heaven on Earth.
This means we are to have desires; we are to set intentions or a plan for the life we would like to experience. Within the context of these intentions and our plan, we are to be willing to receive this or something better through the grace of God and to the highest good of all concerned. If we do not state our intentions or our desires, we live a life designed and created by others. We wouldn't go into a restaurant and expect the waiter to choose what we are going to eat. If we don't make the choices for our lives, we receive potluck. We get what we believe we deserve and what we focus upon.

List ten things you would like to manifest in your life:

_____
_____
_____
_____
_____
_____
_____
_____
_____
_____

Our souls presume we are focusing on what we desire.

The eighth step to spiritual maturity and happiness is to understand Humans made the concept of money, God did not.
As wannabe spiritual masters, it is our job to understand we should be asking the Universe for the thing we really desire, not its monetary equiv-alent. What do we want to buy with the money? Ask for the thing itself, the opportunity or experience. To ask for the money puts a step in mani-festation that is unnecessary to Spirit. When I was first trying to learn this concept, my guidance used the example, that Jesus did not send a follower to the store with $1.79 to buy loaves and fishes. He just manifested loaves and fishes to feed the people. If you are asking for money to put in the bank to have a savings account to make you feel secure, the thing you really desire is "to feel secure." Many things cannot be purchased by money. The really

important things; health, love, happiness, peace, feelings of security and serenity, cannot be purchased. If we look only to our job, our retirement check, our spouse or our parents as "the source of our supply," we are eliminating billions of other ways God could use to fulfill our needs and desires. If we believe we have to work for everything we get and that it will only come in the form of our paycheck, this limits the soul to only being able to give us supply through that one source. If we really "get" GOD IS THE SOURCE OF MY SUPPLY, then this can be our reality. God is the Source of everything. It gives the soul freedom to bring us our heart's desire through any means it chooses as being karmically correct for us.

Once we state a desire and release it to the soul deliberately, if it is to our highest good, it will be fulfilled in divine timing. If it is not to our highest good, it will be delayed or replaced by a better choice than what we conceived. If we have released it with the affirmation: "I now accept this or something better through the grace of God and to the highest good of all concerned," we can wait more patiently with confidence. We can spend our time and energy focusing on doing the next single thing to do to be in a state of divine grace.

I find it useful to write down my desires and intentions on lists and I intersperse pictures of these desires in a manifestation journal and on posters in order to keep my conscious mind and my subconscious mind focused on what I desire. Having these visual reminders helps to change my thinking so that my thoughts are truly on what I desire instead of on worry. Worry is misplaced creative thought. We get what we worry about, rather than what we truly desire.

The Universal Law of the Fourth dimension, where Earth and we are now, requires we make our requests in writing in order to give the soul and Angels permission to assist us.

Ask for what you desire not the amount of money it would cost.

If you are in debt, list your debt on one page with columns of the total debt and a separate column for the amount of monthly responsibility. Total each column and at the bottom of the page write: "I now accept being totally debt free through financial abundance." This is asking for a "condition," rather than a sum of money. "I now accept" puts your desires in the present tense rather than somewhere in the future. This statement also eliminates the possibility of becoming totally debt free through bankruptcy. At the time I learned this lesson I was in debt $26,000.00 in credit cards, some of which were at 21% interest. With my income I would never have been able to clear the debt or even keep up with the monthly minimum payment for much longer. Within one year I became totally debt free. I now use the credit cards, but expect to be able to pay the total balances at the end of each month. EXPECTATION is important. INTENTION is important. Remember manifestation happens through DESIRE, BELIEF, EXPECTANCY and GRATITUDE.

God is the source of my supply.

The ninth step to spiritual maturity and happiness is faith born of knowing, not blind faith.

I do not like the idea of blind faith. I am a person who likes to have proof. Working with your soul using the methods suggested here will give you proof through the synchronistic events that will begin to happen in your life.

Most of us came to Earth from a vibrational space higher than the Fifth dimension. The Third and Fourth dimensions are spiritually visible. The Third, Fourth and lowest Fifth dimensions are spiritually auditory. Do not try to retard your vibrations to be able to see spiritually or hear spirit auditorally. Accept spiritual knowingness. If you agree to spiritually "know," more can be given to you by your soul than if you demand to see or hear spiritually. Once you agree to know, you can "know" a thing spiritually so strongly as to feel you saw it, as if you heard it, as if you felt it in the palms of your hands or as if you could smell it. Ask your soul at all times:

What is the next single thing for me to do or know for me to be in a state of Divine Grace?

When we ask the soul a myriad of questions about: Where's the money coming from? When is the money coming? How am I going to pay the car payment, electricity, etc? Where is my soul mate? When is she/he coming? Should I move? Should I change jobs? And on and on and on. The soul will be silent or give what seems like conflicting or erroneous information. If we ask only, "What is the next single thing for me to do or know for me to be in a state of divine grace", we are asking for "divine grace", which is a condition rather than a thing. The Spirit will respond with an intuitive suggestion immediately. Be willing to move in the direction the intuition suggests. These are suggestions not orders.

Spirit gives information only on a need to know basis. Truthfully, we can only stand to know one step at a time. If we were given the whole picture at one setting it would be too much for us to accept or to comprehend. We can only take one action at a time and everything is always in a state of fluctuation. Remember, change is the norm. Everything is in constant motion. The next single intuition, inspiration or thought will come into your mind, if you ask this question and focus on your soul for a response. Then it is up to you to act upon that intuition. The thought or response you seem to get from the soul may not seem to have anything to do with the eventual goal one has stated as their desire. But it does have to do with setting in motion events aligned with divine timing. After we surrender the body back to the soul that created our body for its use, the soul sets up events, contacts, etc. like a line of dominoes. If we follow the intuition given in response to this question, one event touches the next and the next as spirit is putting them in front of us.

Often I would follow my intuition to show up at a certain place at a certain time and, when I arrived, seemingly nothing of note would take place. I would leave disappointed. I learned after a while the other person who was to have been there at the same time may not have been listening or may have chosen not to follow their intuition to show up at the appointed time. Everyone has free will; no trip is ever wasted. Sometimes it is as simple as our energies were needed at that particular place at that particular time. Our job is to fulfill the Universal Law of Participation by showing up.

**We cannot gain spiritual awareness intellectually;
it must be experienced.**

In the beginning of my following spiritual guidance, or my intuition, I would always try to make it logical or at least to make it make sense to my mind. I wanted spirit to be efficient. I wanted to be told exactly what to do; when, how and why. I wanted no variables. Through the years, I've learned that spirit is not efficient in the sense that they do not see that the closest distance between two points is a straight line. They would send me over here and then over there and then back over here. When I questioned the seeming inefficiency I was told it was "divine timing" or it was about the people I was to meet along the way. Through the years I have learned to try not to second-guess spirit as often. But I still argue or state conditions under which I would do certain things. We are expected to negotiate, to

co-create with Spirit, not to be pawns or puppets.
I HAVE LEARNED MY JOB IS:
1. TO BE WILLING
2. TO SHOW UP
3. TO LOOK AS GOOD AS POSSIBLE

When we enter a room, people have a first impression about us by the way we are groomed, the way we dress, our posture and the look on our face. If this is pleasing and non-threatening, the energies that move through us can affect the hearts of the people who look at us. If we present a less than pleasing appearance, they will look away or look at us without open hearts and the energies we carry cannot be as easily delivered.

The tenth step to spiritual maturity and happiness is to learn to live harmlessly.
We must learn to understand the law of karma, to know that every action has a reaction, every thought and action has a consequence. If we look at all others as parts of the whole, as parts of God, like ourselves, with the same doubts, fears and insecurities, we can treat them with kindness. We can forgive when they pull out in front of us in traffic, when they behave unconsciously, because in reality they are part of us. We can forgive them as we would a dear friend.

Each person I criticize is mirroring a part of me I don't want to look at or admit.
What if we have been misled by half-truths?

The eleventh step is to understand the Bible is a divinely inspired historical record which has been rewritten and altered many times by people whose objective was to control Humanity through fear.
At the time of the meeting of the Nicene Council, the purpose of taking out references to reincarnation was to serve government and church authorities to keep Humankind in a state of fear and doubt about who we really are. The purpose was to keep us powerless and needy; to make us controllable.
What if we actually are extraterrestrials come to Earth as Humans to raise the vibration and consciousness of the Human species? What if Humans were created by a Divine Plan to be self-evolving by thought through various phases: Homo erectus, Neanderthal, Cave man, Cro-

Magnon, Homo sapiens and now are evolving into a new species Homo novan or Homo universalis? What if each of these stages of evolution was aided by spiritual extraterrestrial intervention? What if the "the star that moved" to lead the wise men to the location of Jesus' birth was really "The Star of Bethlehem," which is the name of Ashtar's command ship? Ashtar is the name of the twelve-entity council of the Ashtar Command, which is the leader of the Intergalactic Federation. What if The Federation is made up of fifty-two different extraterrestrial civilizations attempting to assist Earth in her evolution into being a Fifth dimensional planet? What if Jesus was only one of a series of beings that came to Earth to embody the Cosmic Christ Consciousness? What if He was just a man before his baptism, when the Christ Consciousness Ray entered His body and caused Him to become Jesus the Christ? What if the Cosmic Christ Consciousness is a Ray of Energy coming from the Heart of God that can infuse us all? What if Jesus came to prove the ascension through His resurrection? What if the church and we have kept Him and ourselves on the cross instead of following His example to "do these things and more" ourselves, as He suggested?

At the end of the 1920's when Humans thought they were smart enough to split the atom, the Spiritual Hierarchy had to create an energetic barrier out beyond the Fourth dimension to keep the negative thought forms of Humanity and the chain reaction from splitting atoms from destroying portions of the Solar System and the Universe. So the Fourth dimension is filled with all the negative thought forms Humans have expressed for all those years plus the negative souls that did not have enough energy to make it into the Fifth dimension, which Christians think of as heaven. They have been stuck in the dimension where we and Earth are now. This is partially why it seems we are in hell and there is so much addiction and violence happening.

What if Earth is already in the Fourth dimension, but we haven't noticed it because all of our molecules are speeding up simultaneously with those of the Earth and the clocks? What if there is no hell, but what was perceived as hell was the Fourth dimension? What if the lake of fire the prophets saw were the energies of the Fourth dimension: the energies of fear, greed, doubt, anger and raw sexuality? The energy colors of the first three chakras; red, orange and yellow, swirling together would look like a lake of fire. What if a person dies who does not raise their energy vibration while they are on the Earth, or develop an awareness of spirit, God or an afterlife; where would they be? They would be stuck in the Fourth dimension surrounded my many other spirits in the same state of torment; they would be in "hell", until rescued by Angels through our prayers and divine intervention. What if the reason we are experiencing such a rise in crime, anger, fear, rage and inhuman behavior on Earth at this time is because we are moving through the Fourth dimension? What if we could change it through collective thought?

What if all the children born since 1985 are members of this new species the Homo universalis? What if they have an etheric twelve-strand helix of the DNA and the Homo sapiens who are trying to educate them have a two-strand helix of the DNA? What if they have an etheric four-quadrant brain and the Homo sapiens, who are trying to teach them, have a two-hemisphere brain? What if they can only connect to the frequency of information that has been digitalized and is the reason they can easily relate to TV, computers, computer games, electronic devices and animated cartoons, but not so well with people older than they are? What if this is why they are being diagnosed as having attention deficit disorder?

The twelfth step to spiritual maturity and happiness is to understand we are a part of a much larger organism.
What if this Universe revolves around a Great Central Sun at the center of the Milky Way? What if we are fueled energetically by the energies of our Galactic Sun, which is held in place by the energies of the Ascended Masters Helios and Vesta? What if there is Great Central Sun energy at the central core of the Earth? What if there are twelve Universes making up an Omniverse? What if Earth is located in the Twelfth sector of space in the Twelfth Universe of this Omniverse? What if there is a Spiritual Hierarchy of spiritual beings, many of whom are graduates of Earth, who orchestrate the workings of the Omniverse, this Universe, Earth and all the other planets and galaxies, in accordance with the Divine Plan of the Creator God? What if there is only one God Creator of all Universes? What if each planet and star system has a Planetary Lord? What if the Old and New Testaments were historical accounts of two Planetary Lords and not the Creator God of all Universes? What if the Divine Plan is given down to the Angelic Realm, who pass it on to the Spiritual Hierarchy, who pass it down to the Intergalactic Federation, who pass it on to us Humans through soul intuition contact?

What if there are thirty-seven Fifth dimensional inner Earth civilizations within Earth? What if they are spiritually advanced remnants of the Anasazi, Aztec, Incan, Toltec, Inuit, Paiute and other indigenous tribes of Earth?

What if many people on the Earth have agreed to hold the energies of the Cosmic Christ Consciousness on the Earth at this time? What if we are the Messiah everyone has been waiting for? What if no one person has the capability of holding the amount of Cosmic Christ Consciousness energy it will take to cause this evolution to be successful? What if it takes a group consciousness, a group Messiah and you are a part of it? What if many teams of individuals have volunteered, from many Universes, to incarnate at this time on Earth to carry the Cosmic Christ Consciousness energy?

Spiritual maturity involves being willing to remember. It means waking up from collective amnesia. It means accepting responsibility for ourselves and the state of the World.

The thirteenth step to spiritual maturity and happiness is to agree to give up doubt and fear and to agree to be who we really are in the World.
To be authentically who we were created to be is the greatest gift we can offer God, ourselves and the World. In order to be authentic we must take time for introspection, to know ourselves, to learn and to live by our own truths, our own standards. We must give up fear and be willing to listen to the soul.

We must see that if we know who we are, as aspects of God, we have a foundation for our lives to be stable like a pyramid is stable if its foundation is firm. If we are in denial and our lives are based on what we "have," instead of who we "are," we are as out of balance as a pyramid standing on its point. We will need to attempt to stabilize our lives, shore them up from addictions, relationships, excuses, and possessions. When we get to the truth of who we are, we can stand on a firm foundation of that truth. From that point, we can co-create the life we desire through cooperation with the soul. This life will feel stable, serene, fulfilling and happy. From the place of "being aspects of God working through these personalities" we can do the work we love. We can have the material possessions and relationships we desire. We can know God. We can be truly happy.

REVIEW OF STEPS TO HAPPINESS

The first step to spiritual maturity and happiness is to watch what we are thinking, to practice self-scrutiny, self-appraisal, self-appreciation.

The second step to spiritual maturity and happiness is to take responsibility for those thoughts.

The third step to spiritual maturity and happiness is to realize that manifestation is fueled by feeling.

The fourth step to spiritual maturity and happiness is self honesty.

The fifth step to spiritual maturity and happiness is to realize you originate your feelings and you can therefore change them.

The sixth step to spiritual maturity and happiness is the understanding the only constant in the World is change.

The seventh step to spiritual maturity and happiness is to realize we are placed on Earth to be co-creators with God, to be the architects of our own lives and heaven on Earth.

The eighth step to spiritual maturity and happiness is to understand Humans made the concept of money, God did not.

The ninth step to spiritual maturity and happiness is faith born of knowing, not blind faith.

The tenth step to spiritual maturity and happiness is to learn to live harmlessly.

The twelfth step to spiritual maturity and happiness is to understand we are a part of a much larger organism.

The thirteenth step to spiritual maturity and happiness is to agree to give up doubt and fear and to agree to be who we really are in the World.

13.

Prayers, Meditations Aad Rituals Correct Definition Of Self

I am God operating through my personality for the benefit of Earth, all species of life on the Earth and beyond. This is the truth of who I really am. As God operating through my personality I deserve health, wealth and prosperity. I deserve positive exceptions to always be made in my favor.

PARTNERSHIP AGREEMENT

I, _____, on this date, _____ do enter into an agreement of cooperation with the Holy Mother/Father God of Light.

I agree to recognize The Creator as my Source in all my relationships both business and personal.

I agree to live from the definition, I AM God expressing itself through the personality of _____, for the benefit of Earth, all life on the Earth and beyond.

I agree to live my life intuitively, asking The Creator at all times, "What is the next single thing for me to do or know for me to be in a state of Divine Grace?

I agree to gift a percentage of my monthly income to the physical source that assists me with my personal spiritual growth.

It is my desire to serve the Universe in the following manner:

1.

2.

3.

4.

5.

6.

I choose to be true to myself. I choose perfect health physically, mentally, emotionally, and spiritually. I choose freedom. I choose to do God's will for my life.

I choose to serve the Universe with my gifts and talents. In exchange I accept from the Universe, through the grace of God and to the highest good of all concerned, the fulfillment of my needs and desires.

This contract supersedes all previous agreements I have made with my Higher Self and is duly in force and operating for me now.

Signed: _____ Dated: _____

GROUNDING EXERCISE

This process will take about two minutes each morning and begins to create a cocoon or barrier of protection between yourself and other people and other dimensions, other than the information coming directly to you from your soul. It removes the static. It also protects you from astral plane interference and possible possession by astral entities.

> If you catch yourself behaving empathically during the day,
> Stop and redo the process.

In a standing position, take a deep breath and focus on the soles of your feet. As you exhale, deliberately intention beams of energy about the size of fluorescent light bulbs (or Luke Skywalker's light saber) going from the soles of your feet into the central core energy of the Mother Earth, or see yourself as a tree with roots going into the center of the Earth.

Take another deep breath and, as you exhale, focus on your heart, deliberately opening your heart in love and appreciation to the Earth, to your physical body and to your Oversoul (God, the sky, the Universal Life Force Energy, or whatever vision works for you.)

Take another deep breath and, as you exhale, open the crown of your head and have the intention of deliberately sending a beam of energy, about the size of a fluorescent light tube, from your heart, through your high heart, through the point of your mid-brain into the Cosmic Christ Consciousness level of your own Oversoul. (Send the beam of energy to the Sun or to God, or whatever image works for you.)

Continuing to breathe deeply, begin to swing your arms gently at your sides to and fro, back and front, as if you are pumping energy up from the Earth. After about one minute, change your focus to above your head and begin to pump energy down from your Oversoul. As you pump, you want to also intention pumping up balloons of energy around your body. The first balloon is white and is about twelve feet in all directions from the body, the second balloon, which is pink and inside the first, is about eight feet in all directions from the body. The third balloon is purple and is about four feet in all directions from the body. The purple balloon becomes your personal energy supply, impenetrable by others. The white and pink energy fields are excess energy, which you can afford to share with others. Very few people on the planet are spiritually adept enough to penetrate your personal energy field if you use this system.

SUGGESTED MORNING MEDITATION

I deliberately seal this room on the north, south, east and west, the ceiling and the floor from any negative energy or entity. I send energy from my body to ground myself into the magnetic energy at the core of the Earth to be stable and to strengthen the iron in my blood.

I call forth the Blue Light of protection for myself, my pets, my home, car and my family. I ask to extend this protective bubble of blue light of protection from fifty miles in all directions from my home, protection from high damaging wind, lightening, excessive rain, flooding, hail, excessive snow and ice, fire, tornadoes, earthquakes, theft, terrorism and violence.

I open my heart in gratitude for my body, my Oversoul, my I Am Presence, my Holy Christ self, the Earth, all the animals, plants, minerals, water, fire, air and ethers, the Spiritual Hierarchy, the Intergalactic Federation, all of the Angelic Realm, the Planetary Logos, the Solar Logos, the Sun and the Moon, the Creator God of all Universes.

I ask for the Violet Flame of Transmutation to flow through the cells of my body, my conscious and subconscious minds to remove all limiting beliefs, doubts, fears, judgments, negativity, jealousy and anger. I ask all the cells of my body be healed and transformed to perfection. I ask my body intelligence to normalize the functions of my glands to produce exactly the amount of hormones and other substances my body needs, no more and no less. I ask my body be polarized perfectly between the North and South Poles. I ask that all the static electricity be dissipated, dissipated, dissipated from my brain and body.

I send a beam of energy from my heart, through my high heart and my mid-brain and into all levels of my Oversoul, my I AM Presence, my Holy Christ self, and into the Ascended Master's octave of Light. I ask to have Ascended Master Consciousness.

I connect to my Mighty I AM Presence and send love from my heart to my Mighty I AM Presence. I call forth the Violet Fire and ask this Violet Fire be sent out to all I perceive as imperfect. Thank you,

I give my I AM Presence and Holy Christ Self dominion over my body, my thoughts, emotions and actions. Turning my eyes upward I take a deep breath, hold it at the point of my mid-brain and count 3, 3, 3 and exhale. Turning my eyes upward, I take another deep breath; hold it at the mid-brain and count 2, 2, 2 and exhale. Turning my eyes upward, I take another deep breath, hold it at the mid-brain and count 1, 1, 1 and exhale. Mentally I count backward from 10 to one and sit quietly. I ask my soul what is the next single thing for me to do or know for me to be in a state of Divine Grace? I write the telepathic message I receive from my soul.

THE GREAT INVOCATION

From the point of Light within the Mind of God
Let Light stream forth into the minds of Humans
Let Light descend on Earth.
From the point of Love within the Heart of God
Let love stream forth into the hearts of Humans.
May Christ energy return to Earth.
From the center where the Will of God is known
Let purpose guide the little wills of Humans
The purpose which the Masters know and serve.
From the center which we call the race of Humans
Let the Plan of Love and Light work out.
And may it seal the door where evil dwells.
Let Light and Love and Power restore the Plan on Earth.

MANIFESTATION SUGGESTIONS

"We do not get what we deserve, we get what we believe."
Wonder Woman

It is recommended by Spirit that we write out our desires with as much clarity and detail as we can using the beginning phrase, "I desire, intend, deserve and now gratefully accept." And then describe the desire.

At the end of describing each desire write the release: I now accept this or something better fulfilled through Divine right action to the highest good of all concerned.

When desiring money it is useful to state: I now accept an ongoing monthly passive income of _____ insert your desired amount. I am always totally debt free through financial abundance and always have a cash reserve on hand of _____. I am grateful my wallet is always filled with cash and my mail boxes are always filled with cash and negotiable checks made payable to me or my company.

You can add the word "passive" to income if you want gifts instead of money from your work.

I command and demand my Beloved Mighty I AM PRESENCE to bring me now all of the Supply that is mine by Divine Right.

FINANCIAL CONDITION

To get a clear image of your financial condition list your current financial indebtedness or responsibilities and release your debt to the Universe.

	Total Balance	Monthly Responsibility
Mortgage or Rent		
Car Payments		
Utilities:		
Gas		
Electric		
Home Phone/Internet		
Cable TV		
Cell Phone		
Water/ Sewer		
Subscriptions		

Bottled Water_____

Maintenance_____

Car Loan_____

Bank Loans _____

Credit Cards _____

    Capital One_____

    Chase _____

    Master Card_____

    VISA_____

    CITI_____

    Master Card_____

    American Express_____

    Discover_____

    Department Store_____

    Personal Loans_____

    Bank Loan_____

Insurance

    Personal_____

    Medical_____

    Life_____

    Auto_____

    Renters_____

    Mortgage_____

Taxes

    State_____

    Federal_____

    Other_____

Totals:

I now release this indebtedness into the Universe. I now accept its immediate and complete payment through rich avenues of Divine Substance. I now accept being totally debt free through financial abundance. And so it is!

LETTER WRITING TO THE OVERSOUL AND GUARDIAN ANGELS

A Problem cannot be solved at the energetic level it was created.

You may use this ritual if you have a situation which needs healing, a condition you cannot solve or a person with whom you have no luck communicating in the physical dimension. You are allowed to write a letter as follows:

"To the Oversoul and Guardian Angels of (name) _____;
I ask for Divine intervention for (my relationship with) (healing for) (the current situation for) (name) _____. I ask for healing of body, mind, Spirit and emotion in all dimensions and time frames. Recognizing that I do not fully understand the karmic implications in this situation, I ask the Oversoul and Angels to intervene. I ask for healing from addiction, anger, disease, (etc.). I ask that (name) _____ become aware of their true nature, their divinity, their mission and their Oversoul. It has been promised that if we ask, we shall receive. I recognize by writing these letters for 14 days, and on the 14th day burning the letters, I am acting in accordance with Spiritual Law. I now release this person and their condition to God for resolution. And so it is."

This ritual is the only way for the Oversoul and Guardian Angels to be given a special dispensation to override the person's free will for six weeks to positively influence the person's life. You may do this for addicted individuals, but the exorcism would work best for addiction as most addicted people are periodically possessed and not fighting their addiction for only one person.

This is one of the greatest gifts you can offer another person. You do not have to have their permission to write these letters. You can also write the letters for the Earth or a country, or condition which is present on the Earth.

Write the letters for 14 days. If you miss a day, keep writing until you have 14 letters. When you burn the letters, you release the person to God and ask for the highest good for all concerned. Fire energy assists in transmuting the situation. You may write the letters every 8 weeks, leaving 6 weeks in between to allow the Oversoul to intervene. Many miracles have been reported through the use of this prayer technique. Read your letter and ask yourself if you are doing this out of love for the person or because of your need to control and, if so, redo the wording of the letter and be honest about your motives.

FOOD BLESSING

Little do people realize the value of energetically blessing their food and deliberately mentally raising the vibration of the food higher than the current vibration of their bodies and neutralizing any contaminants in their food. This is especially important if you, personally, did not prepare the food or if you do not know who prepared the food.

Below is a suggested grace to use before eating;

"We thank the Devas who create the plants, animals and minerals for our food. We deliberately raise the vibration of this food higher than the current vibration of our bodies and intentionally neutralize any contaminants present in this food. We commit to use this food for the nourishment of our bodies and our bodies to fulfill the Divine Plan of the Creator and our souls."

FOUR STEPS TO TAKE BEFORE PUBLIC SPEAKING

1. Ground yourself through your feet into the central core energy of the Earth.
2. Open your heart to the Earth and all species of life on the Earth, plants, animals, minerals, water, fire, air and ether.
3. Send a beam of energy from your heart, through your high heart, through the mid brain and into the highest level of your Oversoul that your physical body can stand without your voice quivering or you becoming emotional.
4. Send a beam of energy from your Oversoul into the Oversoul of everyone in the audience. The Oversouls of the members of the audience will intuitively feed your Oversoul the answers to the questions your audience members have or what they need to hear. This way what they need to hear gets spoken through you.

INVOKING THE 49 RAYS OF GOD

I ask that all energy work that is done in and through my body be in alignment with the Divine Plan of the Creator for Planet Earth all species of life on the Earth and beyond. Through the power vested in me by the Cosmic Christ Consciousness, I deliberately call forth the # Ray to calm and transmute this situation. So be it!

TRANSMUTATION

The Seventh Ray: I invoke the Seventh Ray, the Angel Zadkiel, the Elohim and Divine Complement Arcturus and Lady Victoria, the Ascended Master Saint Germain and Ascended Master Lady Portia to bring the Violet Flame of Transmutation, Transformation and Forgiveness into this situation.

CLIMATE CONTROL

Call on the Twenty-first Ray for the Southern Hemisphere call Master Eufaucheia and the Angel Josiah; the Master Oromasis, leader of the Salamanders of Fire, Sylphs, Elementals of Air, Undines of Water, to put out any kind of fires. Use the term dissipate, dissipate, dissipate, when dissipating storms, and collapse, collapse, collapse to break up storms and destroy tornadoes, hurricanes and tsunamis. Ask for no hail and gentle rain. Claim the energies of all storms and transmute the energies using the Violet Flame of Transformation.

In the southern hemisphere invoke and activate the 21st Ray from the heart of God and ask the assistance of the Master Eufaucheia and the Angel Josiah to do the same things as above.

MAGMA CONTROL

The Twentieth Ray of Earth Magma Control which is the Opalescent Royal Blue Ray: I invoke the Angel Godfrey, the Master Latinaous to control the energy of the magma of the Earth to disperse the pressure build up which can cause earthquakes or volcanic eruptions.

POLLUTION CLEARING

The Twenty-second Opalescent Ray of Emerald Fire may be invoked to purify polluted conditions of water, air and the minds of people. Invoke the Angel Jophiel and the Master John the Beloved.

PRAYER OF EXORCISM

Through the authority vested in me by the Cosmic Christ Consciousness, I deliberately call forth to the energy of the Archangel Michael and the Band of Mercy (a group of Angels whose job it is to move lost souls out of the astral plane) to enter the body, home, automobile and place of work of (name)_____ to remove all negative influences and entities. I ask that these energies and entities be taken into the Light for transmutation and that there be no negative side effects (physical, mental or emotional) to _____'s body. I ask that her/his body now be triple sealed (*it is helpful to think of the person in three bubbles of Light – Purple, Pink and White*) against any further invasion of negative forces. I ask the Angels to close any astral openings above or below this property.

SELLING REAL ESTATE

"We now agree the Cosmic Mind knows where the right buyer/steward is for the property at _____. The Infinite Intelligence within that Mind knows where the current owner/steward is, and is now inter-vening in this moment to bring these beings together for the purpose of this energetic exchange of responsibility and funds. We ask for the intervention of Saint Joseph the patron saint of all Earth real estate and the Guardian of this property to bring the perfect buyer/steward for this property now. Both the current owner/steward and the buyer/steward agree the price is right, the time is right and the buyer/steward is the next correct qualified owner/steward for this property. We agree the property/building/home is now sold in the Cosmic Mind of God. As buying and selling represent an exchange of ideas and energy in the mind of Humankind, we decree that it is so and we accept it completely in our minds right now. And so it is. Amen, Amen, Amen, Thank you, Thank You, Thank you.

14.

Cosmic Marriage Ceremony To Become A Balanced Soul-Infused Personality

Spiritually, we are not asked to seek perfection, but to seek completeness, unity and balance to allow the personality to become soul-infused. To become soul-infused requires our offering an invitation to the soul to actually inhabit the body and to move our ego, our personality to the back to allow the soul to actually be the controlling force in the body. In the original configuration, the ego/personality is in charge and the soul, the observer or watcher. When we relinquish control of the body to the soul we, as the personality, become the observer of the soul's actions through the body.

We each contain both male and female chromosomes and hormones. We each exhibit psychological characteristics, which are considered to be either male or female. Within ourselves we create many personality "selves" that handle, avoid or act out those traits. We are projecting into the World our relationship, or lack thereof, of our inner masculine or feminine natures.

Jung referred to our feminine nature as the "anima" and our masculine nature as our "animus." We can either reject our inner masculine/feminine natures or accept them and relate to them deliberately. The inner feminine if ignored, unexpressed or undervalued can come out in shopping binges, addictions, anger outbursts, eating binges or bitchiness, whether the body is male or female. The masculine nature unnurtured, unexpressed or undervalued can come out as addictive, controlling, threatening, violent, moody or overly aggressive. Moodiness—whether coming from a feminine part of ourselves or the masculine part of us—robs us of a sense of meaning, because when we allow ourselves to be ruled by a mood, we put ourselves in a position of being unable to relate. Often we are so busy trying to control others we don't make the effort to control ourselves.

If the opposite sex, whether it is within another, or us, is given dignity and inclusion it ceases to be the adversary. Anything rejected becomes hostile. Any part of ourselves that we reject or repress, rules us in a negative way. Some people refer to these repressed parts of us as our "shadow self." The "shadow selves" are those repressed or unlived parts, sides of a person's total potential. Often, because of fear, we will keep our creative selves in the shadow, not allowing it free expression. What we don't want to claim in ourselves, we will attract someone else to us who will act out the unclaimed parts of ourselves.

If we are female, we can remain centered in our feminine identity and consciously use our masculine energy (or consciousness) in a deliberate way when it serves us, or we can integrate it and have it available to us at all times. With the integrated self we are <u>less likely</u> to be looking for someone to fulfill this role for us; unless we are still living out the myth of the Cinderella syndrome. And the same is true of a male. This does not mean as soul-infused, integrated beings we won't have male/female relationships. Integration gives greater potential for these relationships to be between two people who are whole and integrated within themselves and with their soul present in their bodies to have the relationship. Until we balance the male/female within ourselves we will attract inappropriate partners or no partners. Our society is not based in this reality. Our society is based on myths. We must become our own role models. To find out whom we are within our male/female aspects we often have to go through a period of celibacy and deep introspection.

We are taught to look outside ourselves for fulfillment. We are encouraged to stay in a state of dissatisfaction. Our dissatisfaction is encouraged and sustained for the greater benefit of those in control. If we do not feel complete within ourselves we are more likely to feel jealousy. Our media, church and governments are designed to keep us in a state of sexual frustration and guilt. The media advocates, "buy our products and they will make you OK, attractive, or superior." We are encouraged to "make love and romance," to be "in love," but not to "be" love. We haven't understood ourselves well enough to trust ourselves to know what is good for us. We have been fed myths and fairy tales as children and taught to role-play, not to be integrated, authentic and responsible. We have been taught to have unreal expectations of others and ourselves.

We, especially at this time in Human evolution, are expected (by our souls) to seek to be interdependent, synergistic within ourselves and with others. We are expected to become consciously synergistic between our masculine/feminine selves and to synchronize our right brain/left brain functions to become whole brained. When we are balanced we can then deliberately invite more of the soul to inhabit our bodies. Then the true trinity is established. The new symbol for this integration is the modified yin/yang symbol to include a third quadrant to represent the spirit. When we were operating in a duality system the yin/yang symbol was appropriate. Now that we are moving into a new dimension that is not about duality, but about unity, we need a new symbol. If you visually look at this new symbol it is not stagnant, it has motion.

MEDITATION TO EXPERIENCE COSMIC MARRIAGE WITHIN ONESELF

In a meditative state, feel yourself in a beautiful setting of your own creation. It might be a church, temple, beach, garden, or any setting of your choice. Allow yourself to be as relaxed as possible and still hear the meditation leader's voice. You may want to record the meditation in your own voice.

Now imagine (intend) yourself as an image of the perfection of your feminine aspect beautifully dressed for this special occasion. (Pause) When you have a feeling of that presence you may proceed to imagine (intend) the presence of your own masculine aspect, also beautifully attired for this special occasion. (Pause) Once you have these two aspects of yourself present, invite your Oversoul aspect to join you. The Oversoul aspect will now ask each of you certain questions to perform the integration ceremony and at the conclusion of the ceremony will actually merge with you.

"Welcome to this most wondrous, joyful and auspicious occasion, for the purpose of the joining of your own masculine and feminine aspects with your soul in cosmic marriage. I will ask for commitments from each of you. As I ask the questions, if you feel you are able to fulfill the agreement please respond with, 'I do.'

"Do you as the masculine aspect of _____ (mentally insert your own name) agree to be active and fully present in this relationship to bring your honesty, virility, nobility, bravery, strength and stamina to defend your feminine nature? *Wait for response...* Will you agree to be devoted to your own feminine nature with perception, patience, courage, and wisdom? *Wait for response...* Will you agree to use your power, assertive nature and willingness to analyze, reason out, focus and project the ideas given to you by your spiritually receptive feminine nature into the World for the benefit of Earth and all her inhabitants? *Wait for response...* Do you agree to be practical, progressive, compassionate, understanding, playful, sensual, but non-competitive with your feminine nature? *Wait for response...* Will you agree to express your own emotions actively in a loving manner and to cherish and uphold the dignity of your feminine self with respect and humor? *Wait for response...* Do you agree to trust and express the combined logic and intuition of your masculine nature? *Wait for response...*

"Do you as the feminine aspect of _____ (mentally insert your own name) agree to be fully present and active in this relationship with your masculine self, to fully bring your spiritual intuitive receptive nature to this relationship? *Wait for response...* Do you agree to be sensitive, creative, beautifying, delicate, connected and nurturing to all aspects of yourself? *Wait for response...* Do you agree to be completely supportive of yourself and your masculine nature? *Wait for response...* Do you agree to bring grace, fertility and inspiration to this relationship? *Wait for response...* Do you agree to be compassionate, understanding, playful, sensual but non-competitive with your masculine nature? *Wait for response...* Will you agree to express your own emotions actively in a loving manner and to cherish and uphold the dignity of your masculine self with respect and humor? *Wait for response...* Do you agree to trust and express the combined logic and intuition of your feminine nature?" *Wait for response...*

"In answering these requests in the affirmative, you have committed to conscious participation of both the masculine and feminine sides of your nature and in doing so I ask you to now embrace to seal this committed union." (Pause) Give time for the energies to merge."

After the male/female aspects embrace in your intention the soul aspect steps forward to embrace and join with the combined masculine/ feminine aspects. The cosmic marriage establishes the holy trinity within you. The vortex is complete. You now have the energetic focus to be a balanced, integrated, soul-infused being. So be it and so it is.

This process can also be used instead of the traditional marriage vows.

9 7 8 1 4 2 1 8 3 5 8 5 3